THE AUTHOR

IRVING J. LEE (Ph.D. Northwestern) was one of the best-known teachers of speech in America. In addition to his work at Northwestern he conducted management training programs in many large Midwestern corporations. He also originated a One-Day Communication School for several such companies—a 6-hour study of communication problems by lecture, demonstrations, and case-discussions. He was Consultant on communication problems to the Headquarters, U.S. Air Force, in Washington, and was a Lecturer to the Air War College until his recent death. He was author of *How to Talk with People* and *Language Habits in Human Affairs*, and editor of *The Language of Wisdom and Folly*.

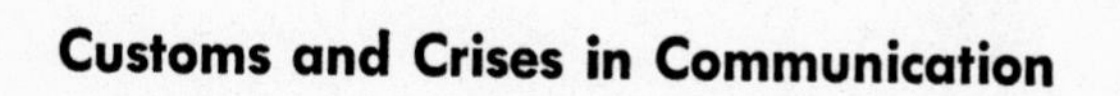

Customs and Crises in Communication

Customs and Crises in Communication

Cases for the Study of Some Barriers and Breakdowns

by Irving J. Lee

Northwestern University

Harper & Brothers, Publishers, New York

CUSTOMS AND CRISES IN COMMUNICATION

Printed in the United States of America

D-G

Library of Congress catalog card number: 54-8594

To the memory of

RALPH BROWNELL DENNIS

He was willing to adventure.

Contents

PART V

PART VI

PART VII

Preface

The important part of this book was written by men and women for purposes very different from those I have here in mind. They wrote to reveal, clarify, entertain, illuminate. Their materials are now offered as cases suggesting something of the nature and variety of breakdowns in communication.

Sometimes there is trouble when men talk with each other. Sometimes there is trouble when they say too little. Sometimes they say it blunderingly. Sometimes they miss what others say. Sometimes they hear but fail to understand or hear and understand too well. All this and more may be found in these cases.

I have observed and worked with a fair number of groups in an attempt to discover the values that come from talking, not about abstruse questions, but about narratives that have to do with the interactions of people. I report some of those findings in the opening section. Among those I found most impressive is the fact that members of a case-group have an opportunity to scrutinize their own communication processes in the very effort to unravel those of others. Often, too, men and women come to see that there is a difference between sitting in judgment on another and understanding how and what he sees, assumes, and feels. They begin with what is easier, judging, approving, condemning. It is only as they mature in their study of others and themselves, that the easy praising and blaming give way to asking, searching, listening. And what is of equal interest for me, it is clear that the class hour can become a testing-ground on which each member can measure the reach of his own arts and habits of communication.

Whether these observations will be reaffirmed in the experience of others is a matter on which prophecy can help but little. It is enough at this moment if teachers are assured that the experience may be edifying, if not enlightening, especially if they have begun to wonder about the effectiveness of their established procedures. For one teacher, at least, the study of cases has sharpened some perspectives and uncovered others hitherto unrealized.

To those authors and publishers who permitted the publication of their material I have a special obligation. Without their generosity this view of the case-method would remain a matter of speculation only.

IRVING J. LEE

Evanston, Illinois
March, 1954

Customs and Crises in Communication

THE history of human thought is the record, not of a progressive discovery of truth, but of our gradual emancipation from error.

—Norman Kemp Smith

WORDSWORTH and myself called on Coleridge when he was living at Gillman's. We sat with him two hours, he talking the whole time without intermission. When we left the house, we walked for some time without speaking.

"What a wonderful man he is!" exclaimed Wordsworth.

"Wonderful, indeed," said I.

"What depth of thought, what richness of expression!" continued Wordsworth.

"There's nothing like him that I ever heard," rejoined I.

Another pause.

"Pray," inquired Wordsworth, "did you precisely understand what he said about the Kantean philosophy?"

"Not precisely."

"Or about the plurality of worlds?"

"I can't say I did. In fact, if the truth must out, I did not understand a syllable from one end of his monologue to the other."

"No more," said Wordsworth, "did I."

—Samuel Rogers

The Case Method—A Point of View

Eton Master, William Cory, wrote these words in 1861:

> You go to school at the age of twelve or thirteen; and for the next four or five years you are not engaged so much in acquiring knowledge as in making mental efforts under criticism. A certain amount of knowledge you can indeed with average facilities acquire so as to retain; nor need you regret the hours that you have spent on much that is forgotten, *for the shadow of lost knowledge at least protects you from many illusions*. But you go to a great school, not for knowledge so much as for arts and habits; for the habit of attention, for the art of expression, for the art of assuming at a moment's notice a new intellectual posture, for the art of entering quickly into another person's thoughts, for the habit of submitting to censure and refutation, *for the art of indicating assent or dissent in graduated terms*, for the habit of regarding minute points of accuracy, for the habit of working out what is possible in a given time, for taste, for discrimination, for mental courage, and mental soberness. Above all, you go to a great school for self-knowledge.

This is one way of stating an educational ideal. It is also a way of pointing to the arts and habits that make for good communication.

Whether the drama of men talking unfolds in harmony or turmoil depends very much on whether the actors have learned to overcome the impulse to inattention and indifference, to oversimplification and exaggeration, to misunderstanding and misrepresentation.

These are no small goals. How can students be helped to realize them? Each teacher will have an answer of his own. In this book I suggest one way of trying the student out, of putting him in a certain kind of classroom situation where he can test his mastery of these arts and the adequacy of his habits. This proving-ground may show not only what he has learned—it may also help him discover what he should have learned. What is even more important is the possibility that the exposure to the testing process may move him to experiment, to try some changes in his own ways of talking.

What Is This Classroom-Testing Situation?

The situation has but four elements: a teacher, a group of students, a room, and a case.

Let us consider each of these in turn.

1. A teacher has two tasks: to see that several do not talk at once, and to help each participant say what he has to say without the teacher's criticism, refutation, or correction of what is said. The teacher's task does not involve lecturing about or explaining what the case means and how the trouble could have been averted or dissolved. He is not expected to summarize, synthesize, classify, define, or analyze the adequacy of what has been or what should have been said. He is expected to do nothing that will hamper the free expression of each

and every member of the group. He may comment on the case but his mood is that of the apprentice not the master. He may ask questions, but his purpose is clarification not examination of the student. He may comment on something a student says, but his purpose is not to expand on it or deflate it. He must be satisfied with putting in his own words his understanding of what the student said, not to support the point, but to insure its expression.

He begins the discussion by asking what the students see in the case, not by asking them to talk about it in any particular way or about any particular part of it. He ends the course by examining the students not on lists of facts or conclusions or theories he has provided on all the cases discussed, but on the range, care, and adequacy of their statements on a new case.

In short, the teacher does not assume the burden of study and research in the cases for the students; he does help to create an atmosphere in which the burden for analysis and synthesis remains with the students. He does nothing to limit the strategies that students bring to their attacks on the trouble in the case. He does everything to assure them by his manner and speech that whatever and however they think must and should find expression as part of the wisdom of the group.

He may, as he listens, conclude that the reservoir of wisdom in the group has little in it, but he will do nothing to add to it himself. He will let the group carry on in the hope that the discovery will also come to them. Unless permitted, how will they ever practice "the art of assuming . . . a new intellectual posture?" The sophisticated may have little patience with "the pooling of ignorance." The teacher, bent on the encouragement of the deepest arts and habits of communication, will recognize that until students themselves see the inadequacy of their resources, they will make only small efforts at stockpiling. And the teacher may, as he tests his own "art of entering quickly into another person's thoughts," occasionally discover that the pool is deeper than the surface ripples suggest.

Members of a group may often have nothing to say. They may be silent because they are confused, unwilling to try out some "foolish notion," reflecting on what has already been said, or because "the habit of attention" is getting a workout. Whatever the reason, the teacher does not himself burst into speech. He remains silent. The wait will only seem long. His explorations of his own "mental courage" will tell the group that the responsibility for learning is theirs, not his, that practice in "the art of expression" is for them, not him.

2. The size and composition of the group are not significant factors. The numbers may range from 5 to 150. The ages may be uniform or mixed. The sexes need not be separated. The status of the members is unimportant, so that supervisors may meet with those supervised, physicians with patients, teachers with students, officers with enlisted men, parents with children, upperclassmen with underclassmen.

Individual members of mixed groups often believe it would be wiser if they met with others of similar age, background, and status, but the success of the testing-operation does not depend, in my experience at least, on the make-up of the group.

3. The meeting-room ought to have movable chairs so that the members can readily turn to see each other. A blackboard is often helpful. Only the usual conveniences of lighting, heating, and freedom from noise and interruption are required. For all practical purposes any habitable room will do, even one without chairs, if the people are willing to sit on the floor.

4. By a case I mean a narrative statement about some happening involving people. The happening itself can take a variety of forms and manifestations. It may have to do with a decision that was made, or one that had to be made, with a difficulty resolved or in ferment, with what people said or failed to say to others, with what they said about anything that led to trouble, with how they interpreted or evaluated anything or anyone, with, in short, how they talked and acted in particular, well-defined circumstances.

The case as written can never include all the details that a group is likely to want, though it should provide those that were available and pertinent to the actions and decisions of the key figures in the situation.

A case that describes a specific set of circumstances that happened at a specific place and time is preferable to one that is purely hypothetical. A distinction should be made between a hypothetical and a fictional situation. Members of our groups approached the stories by Joyce Cary (No. 5) and A. Averchenko (No. 7) fully aware of their fictional character. They were able, nevertheless, to consider actions of the people in the fictional contexts. They did not respond with similar assurance when presented with "made-up" situations that "might happen." These cases seemed too unanchored, even unlikely, to our people. "Why bother with problems which someone dreamed up, when there are so many real ones about?" was the prevailing opinion.

Questions, Conclusions, or Cases?

In orienting students to the use of a case, it has been found helpful to differentiate it from a question and a set of conclusions.

By a question, I mean any sort of statement inviting reply or any broad phrasing of an issue without details. "Are advertising and salesmanship imposing a set of values on American life that are incompatible with the values inherent in the Christian-Jewish religious tradition?" or "How far can the use of unscrupulous tactics in meetings be justified?" or "Does the democratic process protect a group against the wiles of participants?"

By a set of conclusions I mean some answer to previously asked questions presented in the form of a summary, a dictum or prescriptive statement.

Probably no one talent is more valuable in our society than good salesmanship. Everybody sells something—a product, a personal service, a talent. Even at home in your own neighborhood you have to sell your own personality to feel accepted and important in your community. The trouble with salesmanship is that it succeeds best in this age by skillfully blending truth and falsehood so that the customer can't tell the difference. What also happens is that, after a while, neither can the salesman.

After enough conditioning in the art of selling, or the art of acting convincing, or the art of being impressive and influential, a man's personality gets adulterated. Some part of him has turned phony, and even he doesn't know it. Let a man write advertising copy for a certain brand of cigarettes, and eventually he will start believing his own words; he'll begin smoking that brand and really thinking it's better than the others. That's a trivial example, but the same inability to distinguish between the real and the fake will carry over into more important kinds of behavior.[1]

Here is a very brief example of a narrative that can be used as a case.

Sidney Webb had no hesitation in using wiles which some would think unscrupulous. He told me, for example, that when he wished to carry some point through a committee where the majority thought otherwise, he would draw up a resolution in which the contentious point occurred twice. He would have a long debate about its first occurrence and at last give way gracefully. Nine times out of ten, so he concluded, no one would notice that the same point occurred later in the same resolution.[2]

What difference does it make if either of these forms is used?

Some rough answers can be given as a result of observations in the opening meetings of 36 committees considering broad problems of safety and supervision. The

[1] Allen Funt, *Eavesdropper at Large*, New York, The Vanguard Press, 1952, p. 56.

[2] Bertrand Russell, "Portraits from Memory," *Harper's Magazine*, March, 1953, p. 92.

participants were first-line foremen and assistant foremen in three fairly large corporations. It was assumed that they had a more than incidental interest in the topics, but we could not be certain of that. Nor were we able to learn very much ahead of time about the attitude of these people toward the purposes of the meetings. We knew only that 14 of the groups would consider a question, 12 a set of conclusions, and 10 a case. It was not possible to determine whether the members of the groups were comparable in other important respects. Nor did we take into account the skill and experience of the group leaders. Our conclusions must, therefore, be interpreted in the light of these "observational inadequacies." If the reader will apply the necessary discounting these are our findings:

	Question	*Conclusions*	*Case*
1. How closely did they stick to the subject?	Least	Most	Most
2. Were the comments directed to what others said? ("Cooperative conversation" rather than "collective monologue"?)	Least	Some	Some
3. How many people participated?	Least	Least	Most
4. Did people ask questions as well as make assertions?	Least	Some	Some
5. How eager were they to participate?	Least	Least	Most
6. How many "practical suggestions" were made?	Some	Least	Some

	Question	*Conclusions*	*Case*
7. Did they think about the topic before the meeting?	Least	Least	Some
8. How many of the issues considered were introduced by the members rather than the leader?	Least	Least	Most

(Note that decisive differences occurred only in items 3, 5, and 8. Information on items 5 and 7 was obtained from interviews with leaders and members after the meetings.)

If I had to make a series of judgments about each of the forms, I should give the following in the hope that readers will realize that these statements imply indications rather than authoritative directives.

A. A Question

1. Interest and quantity of participation are related to the amount of background and depth of the views of the participants. The more they know and feel about the question the wider is the participation and the more intense the interest in talking about it.

2. The breadth of the question gives the people a feeling of uncertainty as to where to begin and just where to go.

3. The unconfined area of a question encourages people to wander from topic to topic.

4. The open character of a question tends to stimulate people to individual monologues unrelated to the

contributions of others. Men talk in turn. They do not talk with each other.

5. Individuals are often hesitant about getting into the discussion for fear of not making an important contribution. "I'm not sure that what I have to say about it is worth saying" reflects the attitude.

6. A question acts as a beacon to those who have confidence in their argumentative prowess. It is something frightening to the verbally insecure.

B. A Set of Conclusions

1. They set up a battleground on which members take sides, agreeing and disagreeing with the circumference of the dispute limited to the positions as presented. There is some hesitation about modifying the conclusions as presented. They are to be defended or attacked.

2. People wonder why the defender came to his set of conclusions rather than how he can validate them. The discussion becomes a sort of psychological inquiry into the dynamics of belief rather than an analysis of the situations and relationships which form the basis for the beliefs.

3. The amount and eagerness of the participation varies directly with the general background of interest in the subject matter of the conclusions.

4. There is a tendency to assert conclusions throughout the discussion on the same level of abstraction as the original statement. Thus, if no specific illustrations are given in the original, they tend not to be offered by the group.

C. A Case

1. People who hesitate to talk when questions or conclusions are presented tend to participate in the discussion of a case even though the subject is peripheral to their interests.

2. The tendency of the talk to swing between the concrete and the abstract is greater than in the other two. A. Lawrence Lowell's famous dictum that "Dealing with the concrete does not lead to knowledge of the abstract" was made in a context that involved a distinction between a draftsman and an architect, an accountant and a mathematician. In the context of participation in a meeting when a case is presented the dictum does not similarly apply. When people are faced with a concrete case, they may not *discover* abstract knowledge, but they bring whatever abstract knowledge they have to bear in their analyses. And when people work on a case they are more likely to talk about it in *both* concrete and abstract terms than when they talk about a question or a conclusion.

3. A group that has a series of meetings moves more quickly to "cooperative conversations," whereas they are more likely to continue to make the sessions a "collective monologue" in the question and conclusion sessions.

4. If the tendency of the talk with questions and conclusions is toward a generalized oversimplification of the issues, the use of the case stimulates a recognition that "things are more involved than they seemed at first." Participants told us over and over that they "were sur-

prised at how much could be talked about" when their preliminary before-meeting study seemed to suggest that "the thing was open and shut."

In short, if the extent of the participation and the amount of cooperativeness manifested are unimportant, and if the previous knowledge and interest are high, either the question or the conclusion can be used satisfactorily. If, however, the goal is broader participation, with more talking together, even though initial interest and knowledge are meager, the case is the indicated form of the matter for discussion.

Why Do People Like to Talk About Cases?

My own use of cases in both undergraduate and extension classes suggests that a factor of relevance may be at work. Those students seemed to have a sense of the usefulness of talking about the doings of people that they seemed not to have when faced with the necessity of talking on more remote theoretical levels. They had a feeling of relatedness with the human actions that they did not have with theories about those actions. And that often merged into a recognition that implied, "That did happen or could happen to me," or, "It happened to the man in the case, it could happen to me." That in turn moved to a feeling of relevance that, "I ought or ought not to do things like that." It is the belief that the study of people behaving may give clues or models as to how one ought to behave that gives a sense of purpose not apparent when students talked about questions or conclusions.

I ran a number of comparisons in a number of classes.

First a case, then a set of conclusions and vice versa in the same hour and in separate hours with the same group and with separate groups. My methods of observing what happened were neither refined nor controlled, neither decisive, nor reducible to neat categories, but they do support the belief that people get a sense of significance for themselves when working on a case that they do not get when considering a set of instructions or conclusions.

Do Students Learn "Content" in the Use of Cases?

What is the substance, the doctrinal content of a course or hours given over to the group analysis of cases? In a mathematics, history, or biology class there is presumably something "solid" to be learned. When and how does the student take notes and learn some set of facts and definitions in a case-class?

It will do little good to hedge in these questions. What is proposed here is not that kind of learning experience. I am, instead, trying to describe a situation in which students have a chance to put whatever theoretical notions they already have to work in sustained rather than cursory fashion. A military cliché says that "the battle is the pay-off," that there is no way of assessing the countless hours of drill and training except in the moments or hours of action. My interest reduces to an attempt to simulate the pay-off situation. Men and women spend years on the battleground where they talk to and with others. In the heat of the skirmishes there is often neither time nor inclination to think about tactics and skills. In the classroom with a case as the target, the trainees can have a look at how they are doing, how they make assertions, take criticism, appraise "what is possible in a given time."

In short, in the class hour on a case there are no "tell 'em and test 'em" procedures. There is rather the mood that encourages the participants to think about it, talk about it, and think about how they are thinking and talking about it. There is no teacher doing something for his students. There is a teacher setting the stage on which students can practice their parts very much as they have learned to play them outside. In this rehearsal for more serious performances elsewhere, they may see the necessity for sharpening their lines, their characterizations, and their handling of verbal business.

Must People Fight?

In the course of some years in the field of speech, I have taught courses in discussion, coached debating teams, and judged contest debates. I have served as moderator on radio programs where distinguished men and women considered questions of large significance, and I have been a participant and chairman in symposia at meetings of professional and civic groups.

My more recent experience as a teacher of case-classes, however, has highlighted one important difference. The difference, I think I see, centers around the word "contest."

In the debates and symposia people seemed bent on attacking people. Unless the issues were sharply drawn and stated in oppositional terms, things seemed to fall flat. The sense of battle, of search for the means to supremacy, of driving the other fellow into a corner, were not only present, they were to be stimulated if absent. The setting of protagonist with antagonist by its very design promoted the tactics of combat. The athletic contest with all its emphasis on small gains, on employments of ruse and cunning, on conquest, became the unwitting model of the verbal performance. The mood, in brief, was one of tension and attack, of interpersonal pressure and excitement.

In the case-classes there seemed to exist much less motivation toward the athletic. When members focused on what had happened, how an impasse arose, what relationships led to what, the impulse to domination of man by man in the group seemed somehow of less importance. The drama, moving around the group and on to the case, rarely moved to sustained contests within the group. I never led a case-discussion in which individuals did not differ with each other, but there was no one in the room whose job was perceived as the encouragement of that differing. The distinction between a chairman who permits the assertion of varying views and one who exploits them for the tension and excitement values may not be precisely measured, but it is readily to be observed.

I have no adequate theory to account for it, but the combination of a case about human beings in trouble, students studying the case, and a teacher interested in the encouragement of new intellectual postures, is invariably a situation in a low key, with lessened tension and combativeness.

The most apparent value of this combination seems

to lie in the fact that students can get interested in analyzing a case without the interest that derives from planned and promoted conflict. And this suggested some explorations that are now in only the beginning stages. What would happen if a case-class were formed of people who held firm conclusions on some issue on which they were sharply at odds with each other? Under the influence of the low-key atmosphere would they behave differently? I have helped observe 4 series of meetings of 5 different groups. In each one a team wrote up a case in which the issue was embedded in the interactions of people. The cases ran from two to five typed pages. I was the noncriticizing teacher in all the meetings of four of the groups. On one point only am I confident: they sat through the sessions focused more on the cases than on each other. They did not come to harmony and unanimity on the reasons for the trouble and on the solutions that were required, but they did find it possible to talk without the feeling that the talk was fruitless. I am sure that if they had met to discuss *their* differences, the mood of continuous scrutiny of the case would have given way to the usual attacks on each other. I am not a defender of the faith that a case-session contains both solvent and panacea for human conflict. I should prefer to say that in the low-key atmosphere where the case is the target and the teacher the noncritical catalyst people talk about the case rather than at each other.

Do Members in a Case Group Change in Any Way?

Thirty-nine members, selected at random from seven case-groups, were interviewed in an attempt to find what they "got out of the experience." Most of them had difficulty verbalizing this. Eleven of them were not sure they could point to anything concrete. The remainder gave a wide variety of answers ranging from, "I found that I was thinking hard for the first time in years," to "I realize how many kinds of communication problems people have." One item was mentioned more often than any other: the class was interesting. Many said they never noticed the clock, the time went so swiftly. Some believed that this kind of class never could be boring or dull.

Doubtless this sort of effect has its values. If students, both undergraduate and extension, can be interested in anything, the by-products may be both direct and indirect. They may be moved to study the communication process more deeply. They may even carry the feeling of stimulation over to their other studies.

Were there any other effects? We took our cue from John Ruskin's dicta: "You do not educate a man by telling him what he knew not, but by making him what he was not. . . ." "Education does not mean teaching people to know what they do not know—it means teaching them to behave as they do not behave."

Do people in a case-class develop patterns of behavior that can be pointed to? Do they change their ways of talking as the sessions go on?

I now know that it is much easier to ask such questions than to answer them. After a number of fruitless efforts to pin down some particular narrow segment of response we settled on a fairly broad complex that we called "dismissal reactions." Two members of a group available for study were "trained as observers." They were to record all the modes of talking, gesturing, and acting in which one person dismissed, rejected, disregarded, refused to consider, put aside, or pooh-poohed what another said. They were also to keep, as best they could, a running count of the number of such reactions made by each person in the group. They were to make these counts in the two opening, two middle, and two final meetings.

The analysis of the observations suggests that this kind of research needs much refinement in method before generalizations are justified from the data. The observers were agreed just less than half the time on the number and form of the dismissal reactions. They were widely apart on almost a third of their tabulations. Since the discussions were not recorded there is no way of checking back. We have some reason to believe that if both observers could hear the sessions a second or third time they might report differently.

Nevertheless, in spite of these inadequacies, the observers agreed on two things:

1. No individual was judged to have shown a fixed set of dismissal reactions in the six meetings.

2. The total number of dismissal reactions in the group fell steadily from the opening to the final meeting.

I report these crudely fashioned conclusions because they confirm my own impressions about what happens to people in case-classes. (Critical readers will be justified in believing that this is a reason why the conclusions ought not be reported.) I feel rather certain that careful studies will not deny the point that experience in talking about cases does develop some of the following:

1. People differ, but they do so less sharply. They do not say that another "makes no sense whatsoever."

2. A person may take no stock in what another says, but he tends to present his own view for what it is worth without first saying, "I don't agree with that."

3. A person is more likely to dispense with epithets as he expresses his disagreement. He is less likely to say that another's view is "old-fashioned," "radical," "uninformed," and more likely to replace the name-calling with a more extended exposition.

4. People interrupt each other much less often. A person who expresses an unpopular view is permitted to finish before another breaks in.

5. Before a person's position is dismissed there is a tendency to ask for clarification.

6. Dismissal reactions tend to be prefaced or qualified by an explanation or polite apology, e.g., "I see K's facts, but my experience led me to some which were very different"; "I am sorry that I cannot see K's proposal. I would want to do something much less risky."

What do these reactions mean? As I see it they represent a mood in which members of a group can become aware of each other as joint explorers, rather than as opponents. The quality of the relationship between two persons when one has "dismissed" the other is far different in terms of mutual respect from what happens when he replies in less disagreeable forms. This may seem a small matter, but if the dismissing were not dissolved, in time the group might be. The spiral of attack and defense would grow with increasing intensity.

It must be noted that the new reactions are not imposed by the admonitions of the teacher. They mature in the course of the group's development. They represent changes in behavior that emerge in the circumstances of the discussion. They are learned rather than taught. I would thus rephrase Ruskin. "Education in a case-class does not involve any direct effort by one person to teach others what they do not know—it means the organization of the group's effort on a case so that each may learn to behave as he does not behave in the beginning."

How Much Must Students Know?

It has been argued that psychologists would do well to think about a theory of learning that applies to a person's general education:

Some insist that a well-developed theory is a necessary preliminary stage before one can apply his knowledge to any practical concrete problem. This is typical of ivory-tower intellectualism which completely disregards the facts of history and current living. We all make our adjustments from day to day without really knowing what we are doing in theory. Actual practice in many areas often precedes the development of theory.

The late President Lowell pointed out in his address at the Harvard Tercentenary that the explicit theory of government based on the separation of legislative, judicial, and executive powers was the starting point for the British Parliamentary system after which our Constitution was modeled. However, the successful operation of government cannot in fact abide by the theory. The adaptability of governmental functions to the demands of our culture in the face of an explicit but inadequate theory of operations is a remarkable demonstration of government on an implicit, unverbalized theory. As Lowell said, "With men, as with animals, a continual conscious adaptation to immediate objects may sometimes, if conditions are favorable, lead to a fully self-consistent and harmonious system which to the authors is quite unforeseen, and which is not only very different from, but even quite inconsistent with, the theories that they retain continuously throughout the process."

I am not here proposing that we dispense with theory-making. Indeed, I am proposing that a satisfactory learning theory is what we now lack and need to devise. But in the absence of that theory we need not sit idly by, for it is partly by the very processes of trying to make "continual conscious adaptations to immediate objects" that a theory emerges. In other words, action leads to theory, and theory in turn suggests more fruitful ways of acting.[3]

This position is directly applicable to the experience in a case-class. In the early meetings, it is admitted, many participants do not see much. Indeed, it is not unusual to have someone proceed to "wrap the whole thing up" in a single three- to five-minute statement. Occasionally, a majority will concur. But most often the seeming simplicity is revealed as the creation of those with limited perspectives. In one group, after 22 different cases had been talked over, we went back to the three that had been assigned for the first three class meetings. An observer had tabulated the number of "big points" that had been considered noteworthy in

[3] F. K. Berrien, "General Education and Psychology," *School and Society*, June 9, 1951, p. 354.

the early sessions and the time given to them. On the second time around only one-third of the original issues were considered, and those with quite divergent content. The remainder of the issues were "new." If this is at all an accurate representation of what happens, it means that these students had made conscious adaptations to the facts and that they had evolved "new" theoretical schemes as they went along. It is, of course, fairly certain that there were formulations still available that they had not grown into. And it is conceivable that the talk could have been richer if they had known of them. I am, however, unwilling to overlook the growth that did take place. I should consider the dismissal of what did happen just as inexcusable, as the neglect of the possibility that more might have happened. In any event, the full recognition that the making and learning of theories is somehow related to or even connected with the exposure and acquaintance with data or empirical situations may make for mutual enrichment.

A number of my colleagues, after sitting through one or two hours in my experimental case-classes, had reservations about the lack of background preparation of the students for their consideration of the complexities of the cases. As one put it, "These people do not have concepts with which to work on what is happening to the people in the case. They're somewhat like the man who would look for syphilis without knowing about the Wassermann test." He was in his own way restating a view of L. J. Henderson:

> In order to talk about a topic it is necessary to have an adequate conceptual scheme, a way of relating some things to others, a working hypothesis, a frame in which your

thought is set and in which you may operate on the facts. For instance, if we see an eclipse, we have no difficulty in thinking about it, because we have a conceptual scheme of the moon passing in front of the sun. Not so a savage.[4]

It will not do to disregard this opinion that without some diagnostic formulae at hand students will not be able adequately to think and talk about what is happening in the case. Indeed, its very persuasiveness is one way of explaining why the use of cases today is most widely apparent in graduate schools of business and public administration, social work, law, and medicine. Graduate students, it is argued, are equipped with conceptual schemes; undergraduates must still acquire them.

Furthermore, in the history of science there are many illustrations of the fact that the possession of a theoretical scheme enables one to understand "facts" otherwise inchoate. Charles Darwin wrote this in a letter:

> In October 1838, that is, fifteen months after I had begun my systematic enquiry, I happened to read for amusement Malthus on population, and, being well prepared to appreciate the struggle for existence which everywhere goes on from long-continued observation of the habits of animals and plants, it at once struck me that under these circumstances favorable variations would tend to be preserved, and unfavorable ones to be destroyed. The result of this would be the formation of new species. Here then I had at last got a theory by which to work.[5]

[4] "Science, Logic and Human Intercourse," *Harvard Business Review*, April, 1934, p. 317.

[5] F. Darwin (ed.), *Life and Letters of Charles Darwin*, New York, D. Appleton Co., 1888, p. 183.

But is it not true that the theory which Darwin evolved after reading Malthus was related to his "systematic enquiry" into facts? Could one not argue that the theory via Malthus might not have been meaningful had Darwin not had some *prior* backlog of factual experiences for which the theory was pertinent?

It should also be noted that a group of students, no matter at what level, will have some schemes, and some will have more and richer ones than others. What my colleagues were aware of was this: the students did not all have the range of theoretical perceptions that *they* had. Of course this was true. But again it must be said the discussion of cases is intended to produce autonomous, self-critical behavior in the students, not imitated parrotings of notions that never were evolved from their union of theory *and* experience.

Can Cases Be Used as Instruments of Discovery?

I have up to now been considering the use of cases as a means of testing how students evaluate and talk. What would happen if cases were used as the means of analyzing the efficiency of communication operations in a particular organization? If a group discovered sources of difficulties in cases, could they proceed to codify them as a basis for improvement in their daily performances?

The Director of Training of the Bayn Company was persuaded that little might be lost if we set up a training project with these questions in mind. Twenty-three men and women whose assignments were roughly classified as "middle management," i.e., assistant department heads, chiefs of sections, etc., were invited to attend a series of twelve meetings of one and a half hours each. This group was concerned with administrative activities in the broadest sense. The handling of correspondence, the issuing of memoranda and instructions, and the implementing of instructions from their supervisors constituted the important part of their daily tasks.

We settled on "The Prevention of Irritations" as the goal of the project. It was assumed that anything that was involved in a supervisor's feeling of irritation would decrease his effectiveness and complicate his relations with his co-workers. I should note that this was an assumption that had not been verified. We simply took it as something that sounded plausible and that might well be the case.

The first two meetings were spent discussing cases, distributed ahead of time, so as to introduce the method and point of view.

In the two weeks before the third meeting each member was to write up at least two cases in which he became irritated in communication situations. Fictitious names might be used, but the situations were to be real ones. Where possible, copies of correspondence or memoranda were to be appended. In the third meeting the group, organized into subcommittees, selected the fifteen most widely recurring and relevant situations. These were reproduced and distributed.

The following seven sessions were given over to discussions of the file. In the final two sessions an effort was made to summarize from the cases and the discussions the most important sources of irritation. The results appear as the following communication check list.

The Supervisor as Sender

1. Will what I say promise to economize or add to his effort? Will he have to puzzle out his answer and my statement of the problem?
   a. Did I tell him enough? Did I spell it out for him or is he going to have to find it out for himself?
   b. Did I take 100 words to say what could have been said in 50—or less?
   c. Did I use high-sounding, complicated expressions when I could have said it simply in nontechnical terms? Did I use informal language instead of the more precise technical terms?
2. Did I answer every question he asked—or just the first one?
3. If I have to say no, have I explained why, so that he may see the reasonableness rather than the abruptness and arbitrariness of my answer?
4. Did I hedge on the data or the advice I gave him? If I did, will he then act on my incomplete or uncertain answer as if it were adequate? And then who will get into trouble?
5. Is there any possibility that he might take what I say in a way I should not want him to?

The Supervisor as Receiver

1. Have I given the writer half a chance? In comparison to the time it took him to write it, how much time have I taken to read and think about it?

2. If I am irritated after reading his paper or listening to him, what set me off—some grammatical construction or strange personal mannerism or something equally trivial? And should I not laugh off my irritation if I get what he is driving at?
3. How sure am I that I know what he means? Is it at all possible that he means anything except what first occurs to me? Will time and tempers be saved in the long run if I inquire by phone or memorandum now?

In the course of a letter to me four months after the last meeting the Director of Training said,

> Certain effects have been reported to me from our little experiment. I have talked with those who attended at least eight of the sessions and while they are not uniformly agreed as to the value, the following were mentioned:
>
> 1. They were surprised at the extent of the effects of little things.
> 2. They did not fully realize that what irritated them also irritated other people.
> 3. They were interested in the fact that so many troublesome situations might be dealt with by so few items in the check list.
> 4. They think they might be more careful in the future.

Whether or not the results of this particular effort were worth the time spent is a question that the Bayn group will ultimately have to answer. And whether that group could have come up with a similar check list without going through the case discussions is a question that I cannot answer. Nevertheless, this one experience does let me say that if a group will undertake this sort of effort they will come face to face with matters in the concrete and they will see sharply what had hitherto been blurred. I am quite willing to believe that the check list, without the cases as a base, would be less meaningful and less influential in terms of behavior. Since it was derived by the people from their own experience, it cannot be dismissed as something inapplicable to them.

What Do People Talk About When They Consider Cases?

We began the answer to this question by studying the content and pattern of our discussions so as to catalogue the elements, both unique and recurring, in purely taxonomic fashion as if we were botanists with a large number of familiar and unfamiliar plants.

The broadest categories were these:

1. People talked about the details of the case and the relationships between them as given in the printed page.
2. They made inferences concerning why the happenings occurred and what might follow from them, inferences as to what the motivations of the people were, and inferences about details and relationships not presented.
3. They gave illustrations and analogies from their personal experiences or reading to support conclusions and generalizations about what happened and why.
4. They expressed their personal feelings about the individual's actions and assertions in the cases.

It is an interesting hypothesis to suggest that the character of any discussion is somehow related to the ratio of these elements. Is a session in which the expression of feelings predominates considered by the members as satisfying as one that focuses on the given details? Will members uncover more of what is involved if they emphasize their inferences and conclusions instead of expressing their feelings about what happened?

The present state of our research permits little more than some rough, tentative conclusions.

1. In the early stages of a case-class there seems to be more of 2 and 4 than 1 and 3.
2. As a group gets used to the experience of working on cases 1 and 2 become numerically noticeable.
3. When the group tackles a case with interest and assurance all four modes appear.

My view as of this moment in that a group whose experience with cases has matured will do 1 and 2 carefully and 3 and 4 readily without self-consciousness.

Did the people in our classes attack the cases in any well-defined pattern? We found very great variations in the order and emphasis they gave the various aspects of the cases from day to day. We were unable to predict how a particular group would react to a particular case at any particular phase of the case-course. Most of the observers and I had been oriented to believe that a case should be attacked in a rather "logical" way, i.e.,

First: What is the problem?
Then: How and why did it arise?
Finally: What should be done about it?

Students might be coached to talk along such a pattern, but we were somewhat surprised to find that when left to themselves they did not. This is not to say that the talk was formless, but that it tended to focus on these aspects in all the possible combinations. Then, instead of expecting the talk to follow some predetermined or desired order, we found it useful to note the various areas on which the discussion was spotlighted. We became able to distinguish areas around which attention was centered, in each of which the 3 "logical elements" were sometimes found. This experience suggests that these spotlighted areas may be peculiar to what people see in communication situations that might well not be seen if they were analyzing cases with different content.

I. The content of the sender's message
   a. Just what was said? Is the group agreed on this?
   b. Do we have all or only some of it in the written version of what happened?
   c. Were facial expressions, gestures, vocal intonations indicated or implied?
   d. Do we have the message directly transcribed or reported second-hand?

II. The character of the sender's message
   a. Was it written or spoken or both?
   b. How long was it?
   c. Was it simple, clear, ambiguous, complicated, technical, formal, informal?
   d. Was it accurate, precise, distorted, oversimplified, garbled?
   e. Did these factors (II a, b, c,) have anything to do with the situation that developed?

III. The circumstances or setting of the communication situation
   a. Did the interaction take place in an office, shop, home, field, face-to-face, over the telephone or loud speaker, or where and how?
   b. Did the nearness or remoteness of the people involved make any difference?
   c. Was the occasion one that encouraged the people to be relaxed, tense, excited, worried, afraid?
   d. Was the amount of time taken a factor?

IV. The sender
   a. Of what significance is his status (as underling, equal, boss, newcomer, old hand) in relation to the receiver of the message?
   b. What prior assumptions, attitudes, opinions, feelings did he have toward the situation and the receiver?
   c. What did he see and assume that moved him to talk or write as he does?
   d. Was there anything in his "personality structure" or in his "style of life" that influenced his talking and writing in this situation? Is he "in character" or is he behaving in unusual fashion at the moment?

V. Institutional pressures in the situation
   a. Were there any written rules or directives that governed the sender's or receiver's behavior in this situation?
   b. Were there any unwritten customary procedures or codes that were involved in what the sender or receiver did? Were they behaving in accordance with any institutional norms or pressures?

VI. The content of the message as received
   a. What did the receiver "get" from the sender? All or only some of the message sent?
   b. Did the receiver understand or misunderstand the sender's message? How was this response related to the factors described in II?
   c. Was the message received directly from the sender or were there one or more intermediaries in the transmission?

VII. The receiver
   a. Of what significance is his status (as underling, equal, boss, newcomer, old hand) in relation to the sender?
   b. What prior assumptions, attitudes, opinions, feelings did he have toward the situation and the sender?
   c. What did he see and assume which moved him to listen or read as he does?
   d. Was there anything in his "personality structure" or in his "style of life" that affected his listening or reading in this situation? Is he "in character" or is he behaving in unusual fashion at the moment?
   e. If he replies to the sender or otherwise acts on the situation, to what extent is it appropriate, adequate, productive in terms of the message and intent of the sender?

Why Have Cases on Communication?

In a time of specialization it is not easy to see what specialists have or do in common. But if the pressures that move men in their separate ways are strong, so are those that drive men to check on each other. There is always the lurking suspicion that as I go my way I may miss the insights that come to men who travel elsewhere.

This book, then, belongs to the tradition of those who search for meeting-grounds between people, of those who are in quest of means by which men may learn from and with each other.

What would happen if students, now blocked by the walls of diverse disciplines, were to study what is involved in communication situations? Would there be value in any joint consideration of the barriers and breakdowns in the very processes of communication itself?

Let us suppose that a group of management people in any business, industrial, or military organization were to meet to analyze cases of communication trouble. Would anything come from the pooling of their perspectives? Would a personnel man see anything missed by a man immersed in sales, production, marketing, transportation? Would the director of training have any understanding of the breakdown, that might be shared or deepened by the understanding of those concerned with supply and maintenance, operations, research and development, public relations?

Or suppose that a group of students from different departments in a university were to study the same communication problems. Would the sociology major throw light on any phases of the situation that might be recognized as revealing by the psychologists, biologists, geographers, mathematicians, economists, engineers, or literary historians?

But why have specialists come together to study communication problems? Might there not be comparable values in a seminar on delinquency, investments, child care, slum clearance—or for that matter on any subject?

I wish to make some arguments for the communication focus. This is one of the few big areas of human concern in which there are no experts. There are professors of ice cream, landscape, architecture, endocrinology, but no professor who takes as his province the barriers and breakdowns in human communication. Go through the pages of *Who Knows—And What?* or *Who's Who* and (unless I have missed it) you will find no man who gives as his field of specialization the study of what is involved when people talk together. There may be all sorts of reasons for that. What I should emphasize, however, is this: That the mere fact that there is a field for study not yet pre-empted gives us a meeting-ground for common investigation that anyone may venture upon, without the feeling of poaching on well-worked ground.

There is a further argument. What does an executive at any level of administration do besides communicate, i.e., read, write, speak, listen?

Think for a moment of any person you know who is a working member of any of the professions—ministry, teaching, engineering, business administration, military service, government service, medicine, architecture, etc. In the broadest possible terms his working day will consist of three kinds of activities under which the minutiae of his duties can be subsumed. They are

1. Direct observations and investigations of the behavior of people, instruments, machines, materials, etc.

2. Symbolizing activities such as reading, writing, listening, speaking.
3. Planning and decision-making.

Some people will do more of one, others will do more of another. But at every echelon of operations the observing, planning, and/or deciding begins or ends in or involves the processes of reporting, questioning, answering—i.e., communicating.

Now is it not conceivable that human friction is somehow related to how and what people do when they are asking, telling, and listening to others?

I am not trying to make a case for the primacy of one set of human functions over another. I am suggesting only that the act of communication may be the point at which sooner or later a host of other human functions begin or end.

There is one other argument, too. Most of us learn the various acts of communication early in life. We talk and listen so readily and easily that the acts are all too soon taken for granted. Anyone can swing a golf club and hit a ball in some way or other. But to play around in par is another matter. A whole complex of skills, attitudes, and postures must be developed and habituated. The golfer who cannot organize the physical and evaluational elements into an effective synthesis remains forever outside the circle of effective performers. We have not yet come to a similar understanding that men do not inevitably acquire the basic skills of communication just because they know how to mouth sounds and decipher marks on a page.

In the chemistry texts there are well-defined procedures for the analysis of the contents of a bottle. The tests for the presence of particular elements and compounds can be stated and learned. But shift the scene to the shop, office, or home. Let someone talk to someone else. Let one of them begin in anger, dismay, or hurt pride. How does the other respond? What is the test for the discovery of the perceptions and feelings behind the words? What is the pattern of listening and replying that precipitates or dissolves them? What is the technique for interpretation and presentation by which to forestall misinterpretation and misrepresentation? It is not necessary to take a fatalistic view about our inadequacies in these areas. There are people in great numbers who have these skills so useful in human interactions. There are men and women who do avoid the obstacles, who do know how to analyze the intent of messages, who do find ways of correcting breakdowns. These skills are not to be learned as a result of anguished editorializing about the fact that science has progressed while human relations have deteriorated. The skills, just as laboratory techniques, must be listed and described, and systematically learned and practiced. It will do little good to wring our hands at the breakdowns without raising them in active efforts at prevention and reconstruction. And if this is exhortation, one finds comfort in noting that railroad conductors still say, "All Aboard!"

Further Readings on the Case Method

There is a growing bibliography on the case method. Teachers moved to experiment with the use of cases would do well to sample the list that follows, if for no other reason than to discover that there is considerable variation both in theory and in practice. Teachers do not invariably use cases in the same way for the same purposes. Nor do they report the same kinds of effects of the classroom experience.

My view of a case-class was sharpened by conversations with many of the writers in the Andrews volume and by the writings of Wallace Brett Donham. I had had the opportunity to observe almost a hundred class hours at the Harvard University Graduate School of Business Administration in 1951. My conversations with some fifty students in classes I visited provided both first- and secondhand experience with the values to be derived from hours spent with cases. It might not be amiss if I say that the teachers I saw might not necessarily subscribe to the interpretation I give of the case method. Readers of the following will be able to make a determination for themselves.

Andrews, Kenneth R. (ed.), *The Case Method of Teaching Human Relations and Administration*, Cambridge, Harvard University Press, 1953.

Berrien, F. K., *Comments and Cases on Human Relations*, New York, Harper & Brothers, 1951.

Cabot, Hugh, and Kahl, J. A., *Human Relations: Cases and Concepts in Concrete Social Science*, Cambridge, Harvard University Press, 1953.

Culliton, James W., "The Question That Has Not Been Asked Cannot Be Answered," *Education for Professional Responsibility*, Pittsburgh, Carnegie Press, 1948, pp. 85–93.

Donham, Wallace Brett, "The Unfolding of Collegiate Business Training," *The Harvard Graduates' Magazine*, March, 1921, pp. 333–347.

Donham, Wallace Brett, *Education for Responsible Living*, Cambridge, Harvard University Press, 1944.

Donham, Wallace Brett (Foreword by George F. F. Lombard), "An Experimental Course in Human Relations in Harvard College," *The Journal of General Education*, October, 1947, pp. 8–16.

Donham, Wallace Brett, "Why Experiment? The Case System in College Teaching of Social Science," *The Journal of General Education*, January, 1949, pp. 145–156.

Glover, John Desmond, and Hower, Ralph M., *The Administrator: Cases in Human Relations in Business*, Chicago, Richard D. Irwin, 1949, Introduction.

Glover, John Desmond, and Hower, Ralph M., *Some Notes on the Use of "The Administrator,"* Chicago, Richard D. Irwin, 1950.

Gragg, Charles I., "Because Wisdom Can't Be Told," *Harvard Alumni Bulletin*, October 19, 1940, pp. 78–84.

Hunt, Pearson, "The Case Method of Instruction," *Harvard Educational Review*, Summer 1951, pp. 175–192.

Learned, Edmund P., "Vandercook Chain Stores, Inc.," *Harvard Business School Alumni Bulletin*, Autumn, 1949, pp. 108–110, 133–136.

Where Do Communication Cases Come From?

There are four basic sources of cases which can be used in a case-class:

1. Situations provided by members of the group
2. Situations uncovered by researchers in an organization
3. Cases used in other case-classes

4. Cases already in print that were written for other purposes

It might well be supposed that these sources are not of equal value. One quickly notices great differences in the acuity and interestingness of materials written by professionals in comparison with those written by members of an extension class or management group. Students recognize that the professionals "say more in fewer words, and that they say it better." Nevertheless, this recognition is not inevitably followed by deepened insights in the discussion of the case. Students who learn to focus on the human interactions soon take stylistic grace or ineptitude in stride.

There is one consideration, however, that should govern the source of cases, namely, the adequacy of coverage. To what extent are the important facets of basic communication difficulties dealt with in materials already in print? In a sense one cannot answer this question without field research. It is only when we have been able to survey, as close to the scene of communication interchange as possible, the day-to-day crises that we will know how realistic and relevant our available materials are. In the absence of such research we are limited by the range of our own experience.

As cogent as this view is, one cannot escape the fact that on the scene research requires researchers who cost money. Only a well-subsidized institution can begin to afford the expense of the travel and time of qualified observers.

I sought to short-circuit this case-factor by attempting to discover from business, military, and public service people I knew, something of their understanding of the kinds of communication difficulties they meet most frequently. From conversations and correspondence the following list of recurring problems emerged.

People do not listen to what they are told.

One person misunderstands what another says or writes.

Not enough time for instruction-giving.

How do you get what you have to say across to those hard-headed know-it-alls?

We get mixed-up in our definitions.

People are afraid to ask questions.

Overheated arguments by people with differing opinions.

Someone forgets or neglects to tell someone else what the latter should know.

How can I learn to boil down a mass of data into a few pages so others can understand me? How can I get my assistants to learn this, too?

Is it possible to criticize another without hurting his feelings?

Why do not my staff personnel tell me more than they do?

Our supervisors do not read memoranda carefully.

Is there any way to get our sales staff to send their reports in on time?

Men make requests or give orders out of channels.

I see two kinds of pests: the fellow who wants information he does not need and the fellow who wants to tell me what I do not need to know.

My section chiefs do not like to make written records of their requests and decisions.

If those I work with were 25 per cent more accurate and careful in what they wrote and read, our outfit would be 50 per cent more efficient.

We have to give certain kinds of instructions over and over. Why is not once or twice enough?

One way to classify these problems is to differentiate those that involve attitudes of resistance or noncooperation from those that involve rather specific skills in composition. Another way is to separate the difficulties that result from acts of omission from those of commission. Still another way involves a distinction between difficulties that stem from attitudes and reactions peculiar to (1) supervisors and (2) those who are supervised. And still another way would consider the problems growing out of the special characteristics of the organizational structure in one category, with problems growing out of the personality characteristics of the personnel in another.

No matter how the classification is made, it will be arbitrary and selective. I decided, therefore, to focus on cases in which the perceptions, assumptions, attitudes, and feelings of the people in the communication situation led to noncooperation, conflict, and misunderstanding. This meant in practice that problems that grew out of the complexities of organizational structure or those that resulted from inadequacies in the elementary skills of writing, reading, and speaking would not be considered, unless they were accompanied by the other human manifestations as well.

Each of the 42 cases in this collection will thus revolve in a fairly narrow orbit of arrogance, egocentricity, misconception, and misinterpretation. This does not mean that they must be so analyzed. In almost every case every possible set of categories can be brought to bear. The choice of cases with this set of emphases is intended only to reflect my understanding of what I have been told and what I have seen of the basic and significant troubles that beset people in the communication process.

There is thus nothing intrinsically unique or essential in these cases. If any research into the day-by-day doings of people uncovers interactions or complications that are soft-pedaled or nonexistent here it should be easy enough to shift the focus and the scope so as to include them.

Why Include Items 43–49?

In almost every group considering communication cases I have worked with, questions have been raised about principles or theories of prevention. "Are there any suggestions or means by which these breakdowns might be guarded against?" is the theme.

The temptation to provide a list of readings or a lecture was strong. After several experiments in submission to both temptations, a suggestion was made in one group that we ought to discuss, not a case, but someone's advice about how to act so as to keep a case from happening. The items numbered 43 through 49 have been extremely useful in stimulating discussion and reflection. They have been most useful when considered near the end of the course.

PART I

Man, proud man,
Drest in a little brief authority,
Most ignorant of what he's most assured.
—William Shakespeare

• 1 •

General Patton and the Sicilian Slapping Incidents[1]

HENRY J. TAYLOR

Headquarters Seventh Army
A.P.O. #758, U.S. Army
29th August, 1943

My dear General Eisenhower:

Replying to your letter of August 17, 1943, I want to commence by thanking you for this additional illustration of your fairness and generous consideration in making the communication personal.

I am at a loss to find words with which to express my chagrin and grief at having given you, a man to whom I owe everything and for whom I would gladly lay down my life, cause for displeasure with me.

I assure you that I had no intention of being either harsh or cruel in my treatment of the two soldiers in question. My

[1] From the book *Deadline Delayed* by Members of the Overseas Press Club. Copyright, 1947, by E. P. Dutton and Co., Inc., New York. Reprinted by permission.

sole purpose was to try and restore in them a just appreciation of their obligation as men and soldiers.

In World War I, I had a dear friend and former schoolmate who lost his nerve in an exactly analogous manner, and who, after years of mental anguish, committed suicide.

Both my friend and the medical men with whom I discussed his case assured me that had he been roundly checked at the time of his first misbehavior, he would have been restored to a normal state.

Naturally, this memory actuated me when I inaptly tried to apply the remedies suggested. After each incident I stated to officers with me that I felt I had probably saved an immortal soul. . . .

Very respectfully,
(*Signed*) G. S. Patton, Jr.
Lieut. General, U.S. Army

General D. D. Eisenhower
Headquarters AFHQ
APO #512—U.S. Army

When General Patton gave me a copy of this letter he lay back on the bed in his field-trailer and said, "What does that sound like to you?"

"It sounds to me like only half of the story," I said.

So, first, let's see what actually happened.

Private Charles H. Kuhl (in civilian life a carpet layer from South Bend, Indiana), ASN 35536908, L Company, 26th Infantry, 1st Division, was admitted to the 3rd Battalion, 26th Infantry aid station in Sicily on August 2, 1943, at 2:10 P.M.

He had been in the Army eight months and with the 1st Division about thirty days.

A diagnosis of "Exhaustion" was made at the station

by Lieutenant H. L. Sanger, Medical Corps, and Kuhl was evacuated to C Company, 1st Medical Battalion, well to the rear of the fighting.

There a note was made on his medical tag stating that he had been admitted to this place three times during the Sicilian campaign.

He was evacuated to the clearing company by Captain J. D. Broom, M.C., put in "quarters" and given sodium amytal, one capsule night and morning, on the prescription of Captain N. S. Nedell, M.C.

On August 3rd the following remark appears on Kuhl's Emergency Medical Tag: "Psychoneuroses anxiety state—moderately severe. Soldier has been twice before in hospital within ten days. He can't take it at front evidently. He is repeatedly returned." (signed) Capt. T. P. Covington, Medical Corps.

By this route and in this way Private Kuhl arrived in the receiving tent of the 15th Evacuation Hospital, where the blow was struck that was heard round the world.

"I came into the tent," explains General Patton, "with the commanding officer of the outfit and other medical officers.

"I spoke to the various patients, especially commending the wounded men. I just get sick inside myself when I see a fellow torn apart, and some of the wounded were in terrible, ghastly shape. Then I came to this man and asked him what was the matter."

The soldier replied, "I guess I can't take it."

"Looking at the others in the tent, so many of them badly beaten up, I simply flew off the handle."

Patton squared off in front of the soldier.

He called the man every kind of a loathsome coward and then slapped him across the face with his gloves.

The soldier fell back. Patton grabbed him by the scruff of the neck and kicked him out of the tent.

Kuhl was immediately picked up by corpsmen and taken to a ward.[2]

Returning to his headquarters Patton issued the following memorandum to Corps, Division and Separate Brigade Commanders two days later:

Headquarters Seventh Army
APO #758 U.S. Army
5 August, 1943

It has come to my attention that a very small number of soldiers are going to the hospital on the pretext that they are nervously incapable of combat.

Such men are cowards, and bring discredit on the Army and disgrace to their comrades whom they heartlessly leave to endure the danger of a battle while they themselves use the hospital as a means of escaping.

You will take measures to see that such cases are not sent to the hospital, but are dealt with in their units.

Those who are not willing to fight will be tried by Court-Martial for cowardice in the face of the enemy.

(*Signed*) G. S. Patton, Jr.
Lieut. General, U.S. Army
Commanding

Five days later General Patton, not a medical man, again took matters into his own hands.

[2] There Kuhl was found to have a temperature of 102.2 degrees F., gave a history of chronic diarrhea for the past month, and was shown by a blood test to have malaria.

He slapped another soldier.

Private Paul G. Bennett, ASN 70000001, C Battery, Field Artillery, was admitted to the 93rd Evacuation Hospital on August 10th at 2:20 P.M.

Bennett, still only twenty-one, had served four years in the Regular Army. He had an excellent record. His unit had been attached to the II Corps since March and he had never had any difficulties until four days earlier when his best friend in the outfit, fighting near by, was wounded in action.

Bennett could not sleep that night and felt nervous. The shells going over "bothered" him. "I keep thinking they're going to land right on me," he said. The next day he became increasingly nervous about the firing and about his buddy's recovery.

A battery aid man sent him to the rear echelon, where a medical officer gave him some medicine which made him sleep. But he was still nervous, badly disturbed.

On August 10th the medical officer ordered him to the 93rd Evacuation Hospital, although Bennett begged not to be evacuated because he did not want to leave his unit.

General Patton arrived at the hospital that day.

Bennett was sitting in the receiving tent, huddled up and shivering.

Patton spoke to all the injured men. He was solicitous, kind and inspiring. But when he and Major Charles B. Etter, the receiving officer in charge, reached Bennett and Patton asked the soldier what his trouble was, the soldier replied, "It's my nerves," and began to sob.

Patton turned on him like a tiger, screaming at him: "What did you say?"

"It's my nerves," sobbed Bennett. "I can't take the shelling any more."

In this moment Patton lost control of himself completely. Without any investigation of the man's case whatever, he rushed close to Bennett and shouted: "Your nerves, hell. You are just a . . . coward, you yellow b—."

Then he slapped the soldier hard across the face.

"Shut up that . . . crying," he yelled. "I won't have these brave men here who have been shot seeing a yellow b— sitting here crying."

Patton struck at the man again. He knocked his helmet liner off his head into the next tent. Then he turned to Major Etter and yelled, "Don't admit this yellow b—, there's nothing the matter with him. I won't have the hospitals cluttered up with these SOB's who haven't got the guts to fight."

Patton himself began to sob. He wheeled around to Colonel Donald E. Currier, the 93rd's commanding Medical Officer. "I can't help it," he said. "It makes me break down to see brave boys and to think of a yellow b— being babied."

But this was not all. In his blind fury, Patton turned on Bennett again. The soldier now was managing to sit at attention, although shaking all over.

"You're going back to the front lines," Patton shouted. "You may get shot and killed, but you're going to fight. If you don't, I'll stand you up against a wall and have a firing squad kill you on purpose.

"In fact," he said, reaching for his revolver, "I ought to shoot you myself, you — whimpering coward."

As he left the tent Patton was still yelling back at the receiving officer to "send that yellow SOB back to the front line."

Nurses and patients, attracted by the shouting and cursing, came from the adjoining tent and witnessed this disturbance.

Patton made no initial report of these affairs to his superior, General Eisenhower, who was then in his Headquarters at Tunis on the North African mainland.

"I felt ashamed of myself," General Patton told me, "and I hoped the whole thing would die out."

But an official report by Lieut. Colonel Perrin H. Long, Medical Corps consulting physician, was already on the way to Allied Headquarters through Medical Corps channels.

"The deleterious effects of such incidents upon the well-being of patients, upon the professional morale of hospital staffs and upon the relationship of patient to physician are incalculable," reported Lieut. Colonel Long. "It is imperative that immediate steps be taken to prevent a recurrence of such incidents."

General Eisenhower received this report on August 17th. His communication to General Patton was sent off that night.

In his message, which Patton showed me, the Commanding General told Patton of the allegations, told him that he could not describe in official language his revulsion, informed Patton that he must make, on his own initiative, proper amends to the soldiers involved and take steps to make amends before his whole army.

"This all happened practically on the eve of a new attack in which I had been written in for a large part of the plans, already issued," Patton explained, "and General Eisenhower stated therefore that he would temporarily reserve decision regarding my relief of command until he could determine the effect of my own corrective measures.

"Then Eisenhower did four things: He sent Maj. General John Porter Lucas to Sicily to make an investigation of the charges, sent the Theatre's Inspector General to investigate command relationships in my entire army, sent another general officer to interview the two soldiers and made a trip to Sicily himself to determine how much resentment against me existed in the army.

"Eisenhower's problem was whether what I had done was sufficiently damaging to compel my relief on the eve of attack, thus losing what he described as my unquestioned military value, or whether less drastic measures would be appropriate.

"I went to see both Kuhl and Bennett," Patton continued, "explained my motives and apologized for my actions.

"In each case I stated that I should like to shake hands with them; that I was sincerely sorry. In each case they accepted my offer.

"I called together all the doctors, nurses and enlisted men who were present when the slappings occurred. I apologized and expressed my humiliation over my impulsive actions.

"Finally, I addressed all divisions of the 7th Army in

a series of assemblies, the last of which was an address before the 3rd Division on August 30th.

"I praised them as soldiers, expressed regret for any occasions when I harshly treated individuals and offered my apologies as their Commanding General for doing anything unfair or un-American.

"Beyond that, except to leave the Army and get out of the war, I do not know what I could have done."

• 2 •

Mademoiselle Lambercier's Broken Comb[1]

JEAN JACQUES ROUSSEAU

One day I was learning my lesson by myself in the room next to the kitchen. The servant had put Mademoiselle Lambercier's combs in front of the fireplace to dry. When she came back to fetch them, she found one with a whole row of teeth broken. Who was to blame for the damage? No one except myself had entered the room. On being questioned, I denied that I had touched the comb. M. and Mademoiselle Lambercier both began to admonish, to press, and to threaten me; I obstinately persisted in my denial; but the evidence was too strong, and outweighed all my protestations, although it was the first time that I had been found to lie so boldly. The matter was regarded as serious, as in fact it deserved to be. The michievousness, the false-

[1] Reprinted from Book I of *Confessions* by Jean Jacques Rousseau, by permission of Alfred A. Knopf, Inc.

hood, the obstinacy appeared equally deserving of punishment; but this time it was not by Mademoiselle Lambercier that chastisement was inflicted. My uncle Bernard was written to and he came. My poor cousin was accused of another equally grave offence; we were involved in the same punishment. It was terrible. Had they wished to look for the remedy in the evil itself and to deaden forever my depraved senses, they could not have set to work better, and for a long time my senses left me undisturbed.

They could not draw from me the desired confession. Although I was several times brought up before them and reduced to a pitiable condition, I remained unshaken. I would have endured death, and made up my mind to do so. Force was obliged to yield to the diabolical obstinacy of a child—as they called my firmness. At last I emerged from this cruel trial, utterly broken, but triumphant.

It is now nearly fifty years since this incident took place, and I have no fear of being punished again for the same thing. Well, then, I declare in the sight of heaven that I was innocent of the offence, that I neither broke nor touched the comb, that I never went near the fireplace, and had never even thought of doing so. It would be useless to ask me how the damage was done; I do not know, and I cannot understand; all that I know for certain is, that I had nothing to do with it.

Imagine a child, shy and obedient in ordinary life, but fiery, proud, and unruly in his passions: a child who had always been led by the voice of reason and always treated with gentleness, justice, and consideration, who had not even a notion of injustice, and who for the first time becomes acquainted with so terrible an example of it on the part of the very people whom he most loves and respects! What an upset of ideas! what a disturbance of feelings! what revolution in his heart, in his brain, in the whole of his little intellectual and moral being! Imagine all this, I say, if possible. As for myself, I feel incapable of disentangling and following up the least trace of what then took place within me.

I had not yet sense enough to feel how much appearances were against me, and to put myself in the place of the others. I kept to my own place, and all that I felt was the harshness of a frightful punishment for an offence which I had not committed. The bodily pain, although severe, I felt but little; all I felt was indignation, rage, despair. My cousin, whose case was almost the same, and who had been punished for an involuntary mistake as if it had been a premeditated act, following my example, flew into a rage, and worked himself up to the same pitch of excitement as myself. Both in the same bed, we embraced each other with convulsive transports: we felt suffocated; and when at length our young hearts, somewhat relieved, were able to vent their wrath, we sat upright in bed and began to shout, times without number, with all our might: Carnifex! carnifex! carnifex!

While I write these words, I feel that my pulse beats faster; those moments will always be present to me though I should live a hundred thousand years. That first feeling of violence and injustice has remained so deeply graven on my soul, that all the ideas connected with it bring back to me my first emotion; and this feeling, which, in its origin, had reference only to myself, has become so strong in itself and so completely detached from all personal interest, that, when I see or hear of any act of injustice—whoever is the victim of it, and wherever it is committed—my heart kindles with rage, as if the effect of it recoiled upon myself. When I read of the cruelties of a ferocious tyrant, the crafty atrocities of a rascally priest, I would gladly set out to plunge a dagger into the heart of such wretches, although I had to die for it a hundred times. I have often put myself in a perspiration, pursuing or stoning a cock, a cow, a dog, or any animal which I saw tormenting another merely because it felt itself the stronger. This impulse may be natural to me, and I believe that it is; but the profound impression left upon me by the first injustice I suffered was too long and too strongly connected with it, not to have greatly strengthened it.

With the above incident the tranquillity of my childish life was over. From that moment I ceased to enjoy a pure happiness, and even at the present day I feel that the recollection of the charms of my childhood ceases there.

• 3 •

A Case Study of Innovation[1]

ELTING E. MORISON

IN THE early days of the last war, when armaments of all kinds were in short supply, the British, I am told, made use of a venerable field piece that had come down to them from previous generations. The honorable past of this light artillery stretched back, in fact, to the Boer War. In the days of uncertainty after the fall of France, these guns, hitched to trucks, served as useful mobile units in the coast defense. But it was felt that the rapidity of fire could be increased. A time-motion expert was, therefore, called in to suggest ways to simplify the firing procedures. He watched one of the gun crews of five men at practice in the field for some time. Puzzled by certain aspects of the procedures, he took some slow-motion pictures of the soldiers performing the loading, aiming, and firing routines.

When he ran these pictures over once or twice, he

[1] *Engineering and Science Monthly,* April, 1950. Reprinted by permission of the author and editor.

noticed something that appeared odd to him. A moment before the firing two members of the gun crew ceased all activity and came to attention for a three-second interval, extending throughout the discharge of the gun. He summoned an old colonel of artillery, showed him the pictures, and pointed out this strange behavior. What, he asked the colonel, did it mean? The colonel, too, was puzzled. He asked to see the pictures again. "Ah," he said when the performance was over, "I have it. They are holding the horses."

This story, true or not, and I am told it is true, suggests nicely the pain with which the human being accommodates himself to changing conditions. The tendency is apparently involuntary and immediate to protect oneself against the shock of change by continuing in the presence of altered situations the familiar habits, however incongruous, of the past.

Yet, if human beings are attached to the known, to the realm of things as they are, they also, regrettably for their peace of mind, are incessantly attracted to the unknown and to things as they might be. As Ecclesiastes glumly pointed out, men persist in disordering their settled ways and beliefs by seeking out many inventions.

The point is obvious. Change has always been a constant in human affairs; today, indeed, it is one of the determining characteristics of our civilization. In our relatively shapeless social organization, the shifts from station to station are fast and easy. More important for our immediate purpose, America is fundamentally an industrial society in a time of tremendous technological development. We are thus constantly presented with new devices or new forms of power that, in their refinement and extension, continually bombard the fixed structure of our habits of mind and behavior. Under such conditions, our salvation, or at least our peace of mind, appears to depend upon how successfully we can in the future become what has been called in an excellent phrase a completely "adaptive society."

It is interesting, in view of all this, that so little investigation, relatively, has been made of the process of change and human responses to it. Recently psychologists, sociologists, and cultural anthropologists have addressed themselves to the subject with suggestive results. But we are still far from a full understanding of the process, and still farther from knowing how we can set about simplifying and assisting an individual's or a group's accommodation to new machines or new ideas.

With these things in mind, I thought it might be interesting and perhaps useful to examine historically a changing situation within a society; to see if from this examination we can discover how the new machines or ideas that introduced the changing situation developed; to see who introduces them, who resists them, what points of friction or tension in the social structure are produced by the innovation, and perhaps why they are produced and what, if anything, may be done about it. For this case study, the introduction of continuous-aim firing in the United States Navy has been selected. The system, first devised by an English officer in 1898, was introduced into our Navy in the years 1900–1902.

I have chosen to study this episode for two reasons. First, a navy is not unlike a society that has been placed under laboratory conditions. Its dimensions are severely limited; it is beautifully ordered and articulated; it is relatively isolated from random influences. For these reasons the impact of change can be clearly discerned, the resulting dislocations in the structure easily discovered and marked out. In the second place, the development of continuous-aim firing rests upon mechanical devices. It, therefore, presents for study a concrete, durable situation. It is not like many other innovating reagents—a Manichean heresy, or Marxism, or the views of Sigmund Freud—that can be shoved and hauled out of shape by contending forces or conflicting prejudices. At all times we know exactly what continuous-aim firing really is. It will be well now to describe, as briefly as possible, *what* it is.

The governing fact in gunfire at sea is that the gun is mounted on an unstable platform—a rolling ship. This constant motion obviously complicates the problem of holding a steady aim. Before 1898 this problem was solved in the following elementary fashion. A gun pointer estimated the range of the target—ordinarily about 2800 yards. He then raised the gun barrel to give the gun the elevation to carry the shell to the target at the estimated range. This was accomplished by turning a small wheel on the gun mount that operated the elevating gears. With the gun thus fixed for range, the gun pointer peered through open sights, not unlike those on a small rifle, and waited until the roll of the ship brought the sights on the target. He then pressed the firing button that discharged the gun. There were, by 1898, on some naval guns, telescope sights which naturally enlarged the image of the target for the gun pointer. But these sights were rarely used by gun pointers. They were lashed securely to the gun barrel and, recoiling with the barrel, jammed back against the unwary pointer's eye. Therefore, when used at all, they were used only to take an initial sight for purposes of estimating the range before the gun was fired.

Notice now two things about the process. First of all, the rapidity of fire was controlled by the rolling period of the ship. Pointers had to wait for the one moment in the roll when the sights were brought on the target. Notice also this: There is in every pointer what is called a "firing interval"—the time lag between his impulse to fire the gun and the translation of this impulse into the act of pressing the firing button. A pointer, because of this reaction time, could not wait to fire the gun until the exact moment when the roll of the ship brought the sights onto the target; he had to will to fire a little before, while the sights were off the target. Since the firing interval was an individual matter, varying obviously from man to man, each pointer had to estimate, from long practice, his own interval and compensate for it accordingly.

These things, together with others we need not here investigate, conspired to make gunfire at sea relatively uncertain and ineffective. The pointer, on a moving platform, estimating range and firing interval, shooting while his sight was off the target, became in a sense an individual artist.

In 1898, many of the uncertainties were removed from the process, and the position of the gun pointer radically altered, by the introduction of continuous-aim firing. The major change was that which enabled the gun pointer to keep his sight and gun barrel on the target throughout the roll of the ship. This was accomplished by altering the gear ratio in the elevating gear to permit a pointer to compensate for the roll of the vessel by rapidly elevating and depressing the gun. From this change another followed. With the possibility of maintaining the gun always on the target, the desirability of improved sights became immediately apparent. The advantages of the telescope sight, as opposed to the open sight, were for the first time fully realized. But the existing telescope sight, it will be recalled, moved with the recoil of the gun and jammed back against the eye of the gunner. To correct this, the sight was mounted on a sleeve that permitted the gun barrel to recoil through it without moving the telescope.

These two improvements—in elevating gear and sighting—eliminated the major uncertainties in gunfire at sea and greatly increased the possibilities of both accurate and rapid fire.

You must take my word for it that this changed naval gunnery from an art to a science, and that gunnery accuracy in the British and our Navy increased about 3000 per cent in six years. This doesn't mean much except to suggest a great increase in accuracy. The following comparative figures may mean a little more. In 1899 five ships of the North Atlantic Squadron fired five minutes each at a lightship hulk at the conventional range of 1600 yards. After twenty-five minutes of banging away two hits had been made on the sails of the elderly vessel. Six years later one naval gunner made 15 hits in one minute at a target 75 x 25 feet at the same range; half of them hit in a bull's eye 50 inches square.

Now with the instruments (the gun, elevating gear, and telescope), the method, and the results of continuous-aim firing in mind, let us turn to the subject of major interest: how was the idea, obviously so simple an idea, of continuous-aim firing developed; who introduced it; and what was its reception?

Introduction of an Idea

The idea was the product of the fertile mind of the English officer, Admiral Sir Percy Scott. He arrived at it in this way, while, in 1898, he was the captain of H. M. S. *Scylla.* For the previous two or three years he had given much thought, independently and almost alone in the British Navy, to means of improving gunnery. One rough day, when the ship, at target practice, was pitching and rolling violently, he walked up and down the gun deck watching his gun crews. Because of the heavy weather they were making very bad scores. Scott noticed, however, that one pointer was appreciably more accurate than the rest. He watched this man with care and saw, after a time, that he was unconsciously working his elevating gear back and forth in a partially successful effort to compensate for the roll of the vessel. It flashed through Scott's mind at that moment that here was the sovereign remedy for the problems of inaccurate fire. What one man could do partially and unconsciously, perhaps all men could be trained to do consciously and completely.

Acting on this assumption, he did three things. First, in all the guns of the *Scylla*, he changed the gear ratio in the elevating gear, previously used only to set the gun in fixed position for range, so that a gunner could easily elevate and depress the gun to follow a target throughout the roll. Second, he rerigged his telescopes so that they would not be influenced by the recoil of the gun. Third, he rigged a small target at the mouth of the gun, which was moved up and down by a crank to simulate a moving target. By following this target as it moved, and firing at it with a subcalibre rifle rigged in the breech of the gun, the pointer could practice every day. Thus equipped, the ship became a training ground for gunners. Where before the good pointer was an individual artist, pointers now became trained technicians, fairly uniform in their capacity to shoot. The effect was immediately felt. Within a year the *Scylla* established records that were remarkable.

At this point I should like to stop a minute to notice several things directly related to, and involved in, the process of innovation. First, the personality of the innovator. I wish there were space to say a good deal about Admiral Sir Percy Scott. He was a wonderful man. Three small bits of evidence must suffice, however. First, he had a certain mechanical ingenuity. Second, his personal life was shot through with frustration and bitterness. There was a divorce, and a quarrel with the ambitious Lord Charles Beresford—the sounds of which, Scott liked to recall, penetrated to the last outposts of empire. Finally, he possessed, like Swift, a savage indignation directed ordinarily at the inelastic intelligence of all constituted authority—especially the British Admiralty.

There are other points worth mention here. Notice first that Scott was not responsible for the invention of the basic instruments that made the reform in gunnery possible. This reform rested upon the gun itself, which as a rifle had been in existence on ships for at least forty years; the elevating gear, which had been, in the form Scott found it, a part of the rifled gun from the beginning; and the telescope sight, which had been on shipboard at least eight years. Scott's contribution was to bring these three elements, appropriately modified, into a combination that made continuous-aim firing possible for the first time. Notice also that he was allowed to bring these elements into combination by accident, by watching the unconscious action of a gun pointer endeavoring through the operation of his elevating gear to correct partially for the roll of his vessel.

The Prepared Mind Is Not Enough

Scott, as we have seen, had been interested in gunnery; he had thought about ways to increase accuracy by practice and improvement of existing machinery; but able as he was, he had not been able to produce on his own initiative and by his own thinking the essential idea and modify instruments to fit his purpose. Notice here finally, the intricate interaction of chance, the intellectual climate, and Scott's mind. Fortune (in this case the unaware gun pointer) indeed favors the prepared mind, but even fortune and the prepared mind need a favorable environment before they can conspire to produce sudden change. No intelligence can proceed very far above the threshold of existing data or the binding combinations of existing data.

All these elements that enter into what may be called "original thinking" interest me as a teacher. Deeply rooted in the pedagogical mind often enough is a sterile infatuation with "inert ideas"; there is thus always present in the profession the tendency to be diverted from the *process* by which these ideas, or indeed any ideas, are really produced. I well remember with what contempt a class of mine, which was reading Leonardo da Vinci's *Notebooks,* dismissed the author because he appeared to know no more mechanics than, as one wit in the class observed, a Vermont Republican farmer of the present day. This is perhaps the result to be expected from a method of instruction that too frequently implies that the great generalizations were the result, on the one hand, of chance—an apple falling in an orchard or a teapot boiling on the hearth—or, on the other hand, of some towering intelligence proceeding in isolation inexorably toward some prefigured idea, like evolution, for example.

This process by which new concepts appear, the interaction of fortune, intellectual climate, and the prepared imaginative mind, is an interesting subject for examination offered by any case study of innovation. It was a subject that momentarily engaged the attention of Horace Walpole, whose lissome intelligence glided over the surface of so many ideas. In reflecting upon the part played by chance in the development of new concepts, he recalled the story of the three princes of Serendip who set out to find some interesting object on a journey through their realm. They did not find the particular object of their search, but along the way they discovered many new things simply because they were looking for *something.* Walpole believed this intellectual method ought to be given a name—in honor of the founders—Serendipity; and Serendipity certainly exerts a considerable influence in what we call original thinking. There is an element of Serendipity, for example, in Scott's chance discovery of continuous-aim firing in that he was, and had been, looking for some means to improve his target practice and stumbled upon a solution, by observation, that had never entered his head.

Educating the Navy

It was in 1900 that Percy Scott went out to the China Station as commanding officer of H. M. S. *Terrible.* In that ship he continued his training methods and his spectacular successes in naval gunnery. On the China Station he met up with an American junior officer, William S. Sims. Sims had little of the mechanical ingenuity of Percy Scott, but the two were drawn together by temperamental similarities that are worth noticing here. Sims had the same intolerance for what is called spit-and-polish and the same contempt for bureaucratic inertia as his British brother officer. He had for some years been concerned, as had Scott, with what he took to be the inefficiency of his own Navy. Just before he met Scott, for example, he had shipped out to China in the brand new pride of the fleet, the battleship *Kentucky.* After careful investigation and reflection he had informed his superiors in Washington she was not a battleship at all—"but a crime against the white race."

The spirit with which he pushed forward his efforts to reform the naval service can best be stated in his own words to a brother officer: "I am perfectly willing that those holding views different from mine should continue to live, but with every fibre of my being I loathe indirection and shiftiness, and where it occurs in high place, and is used to save face at the expense of the vital interests of our great service (in which silly people place such a childlike trust), I want that man's blood and I will have it no matter what it costs me personally."

From Scott in 1900 Sims learned all there was to know about continuous-aim firing. He modified, with the Englishman's active assistance, the gear on his own ship and tried out the new system. After a few months' training, his experimental batteries began making remarkable records at target practice. Sure of the usefulness of his gunnery methods, Sims then turned to the task of educating the Navy at large. In 13 great official reports he documented the case for continuous-aim firing, supporting his arguments at every turn with a mass of factual data. Over a period of two years, he reiterated three principal points: First, he continually cited the records established by Scott's ships, the *Scylla* and the *Terrible* and supported these with the accumulating data from his own tests on an American ship; second, he described the mechanisms used and the training procedures instituted by Scott and himself to obtain these records; third, he explained that our own mechanisms were not generally adequate without modification to meet the demands placed on them by continuous-aim firing. Our elevating gear, useful to raise or lower a gun slowly to fix it in position for the proper range, did not always work easily and rapidly enough to enable a gunner to follow a target with his gun throughout the roll of the ship. Sims also explained that such few telescope sights as there were on board our ships were useless. Their cross wires were so thick or coarse that they obscured the target, and the sights had been attached to the gun in such a way that the recoil system of the gun plunged the eyepiece against the eye of the gun pointer.

This was the substance not only of the first but of all the succeeding reports written on the subject of gunnery from the China Station. It will be interesting to see what response these met with in Washington. The response falls roughly into three easily identifiable stages.

First stage: no response. Sims had directed his comments to the Bureau of Ordnance and the Bureau of Navigation; in both bureaus there was dead silence. The thing—claims and records of continuous-aim firing —was not credible. The reports were simply filed away and forgotten. Some indeed, it was later discovered to Sims' delight, were half eaten away by cockroaches.

Second stage: rebuttal. It is never pleasant for any man to have his best work left unnoticed by superiors, and it was an unpleasantness that Sims suffered extremely ill. In his later reports, beside the accumulating data he used to clinch his argument, he changed his tone. He used deliberately shocking language because, as he said, "They were furious at my first papers and stowed them away. I therefore made up my mind I would give these later papers such a form that they would be dangerous documents to leave neglected in the files." To another friend he added, "I want scalps or nothing and if I can't have 'em I won't play."

Sims Gets Attention

Besides altering his tone, he took another step to be sure his views would receive attention. He sent copies of his reports to other officers in the fleet. Aware, as a result, that Sims' gunnery claims were being circulated and talked about, the men in Washington were then stirred to action. They responded—notably through the Chief of the Bureau of Ordnance, who had general charge of the equipment used in gunnery practice—as follows: (1) Our equipment was in general as good as the British; (2) since our equipment was as good, the trouble must be with the men, but the gun pointer and the training of gun pointers were the responsibility of the officers on the ships; (3) and most significant—continuous-aim firing was impossible. Experiments had revealed that five men at work on the elevating gear of a six-inch gun could not produce the power necessary to compensate for a roll of five degrees in ten seconds. These experiments and calculations demonstrated beyond peradventure or doubt that Scott's system of gunfire was not possible.

Only one difficulty is discoverable in these arguments;

they were wrong at important points. To begin with, while there was little difference between the standard British equipment and the standard U.S. equipment, the instruments on Scott's two ships, the *Scylla*, and the *Terrible*, were far better than the standard equipment on our ships. Second, all the men could not be trained in continuous-aim firing until equipment was improved throughout the fleet. Third, the experiments with the elevating gear had been ingeniously contrived at the Washington Navy Yard—on solid ground. It had, therefore, been possible in the Bureau of Ordnance calculation, to dispense with Newton's first law of motion, which naturally operated at sea to assist the gunner in elevating or depressing a gun mounted on a moving ship. Another difficulty was of course that continuous-aim firing was in use on Scott's and some of our own ships at the time the Chief of the Bureau of Ordnance was writing that it was a mathematical impossibility. In every way I find this second stage, the apparent resort to reason, the most entertaining and instructive in our investigation of the responses to innovation.

Third stage: name calling. Sims, of course, by the high temperature he was running and by his calculated overstatement, invited this. He was told in official endorsements on his reports that there were others quite as sincere and loyal as he and far less difficult; he was dismissed as a crack-brain egotist; he was called a deliberate falsifier of evidence.

Sims Gets Action

The rising opposition and the character of the opposition was not calculated to discourage further efforts by Sims. It convinced him that he was being attacked by shifty, dishonest men who were the victims, as he said, of insufferable conceit and ignorance. He made up his mind, therefore, that he was prepared to go to any extent to obtain the "scalps" and the "blood" he was after. Accordingly he, a lieutenant, took the extraordinary step of writing the President of the United States, Theodore Roosevelt, to inform him of the remarkable records of Scott's ships, of the inadequacy of our own gunnery routines and records, and of the refusal of the Navy Department to act. Roosevelt, who always liked to respond to such appeals when he conveniently could, brought Sims back from China late in 1902 and installed him as Inspector of Target Practice, a post the naval officer held throughout the remaining six years of the Administration. . . .

• 4 •

The Man and the Desk[1]

F. J. ROETHLISBERGER
AND
WILLIAM J. DICKSON

THE personnel of one of the departments interviewed was moved from one building to another. In the new location, because of lack of space, it was found necessary to seat four people across the aisle from the remainder of the group. It happened that there were three women in the department who were to be transferred to other work. These women were given desks across the aisle so that their going would not necessitate a rearrangement of desks. The fourth person, a man, was given a desk there simply because there was no other place for him to sit. In choosing the fourth person, the supervisor was undoubtedly influenced by the fact that he was older than the rest of the group and was well acquainted with the three women. But, beyond that, nothing was im-

[1] *Management and the Worker,* Cambridge, Harvard University Press, 1939, pp. 544–545. Reprinted by permission.

plied by the fact that he was chosen. Now see how this employee interpreted the change in his seating position. He felt that his supervisor evaluated him in the same way in which he evaluated the women. The women were being transferred to other types of work; consequently, he felt that he too would be transferred before long. Two of the women were being returned to jobs in the shop. He felt that he himself might be transferred to the shop; and there was nothing he dreaded more. Having dwelt on speculations like these for a while, the employee recalled with alarm that his name had been omitted from the current issue of the house telephone directory. This omission had been accidental. The house telephone directory, however, constituted a sort of social register. Names of shop people below the rank of assistant foreman were not printed unless they were employed in some special capacity requiring contacts with other organizations. With the exception of typists and certain clerical groups, the names of all office people were listed. The fact that his name had been omitted from the directory now took on new significance for the employee. It tended to reinforce his growing conviction that he was about to be transferred to a shop position. He became so preoccupied over what might happen to him that for a time he could scarcely work.

• 5 •

A Special Occasion[1]

JOYCE CARY

The nursery door opened and Nurse's voice said in the sugary tone which she used to little girl guests, "Here you are, darling, and Tommy will show you all his toys." A little brown-haired girl in a silk party frock, sticking out all round her legs like a lampshade, came in at the door, stopped, and stared at her host. Tom, a dark little boy, aged five, also in a party suit, blue linen knickers, and a silk shirt, stared back at the girl. Nurse had gone into the night nursery, next door, on her private affairs.

Tom, having stared at the girl for a long time as one would study a curiosity, rare and valuable, but extremely surprising, put his feet together, made three jumps forward and said, "Hullo."

The little girl turned her head over one shoulder and slowly revolved on one heel, as if trying to examine the

[1] *Harper's Magazine*, September, 1951, pp. 97–98. Copyright 1951 by Harper & Brothers. Reprinted by permission of the author.

back of her own frock. She then stooped suddenly, brushed the hem with her hand, and said, "Hullo."

Tom made another jump, turned around, pointed out of the window, and said in a loud voice something like "twanky tweedle." Both knew that neither the gesture nor the phrase was meant to convey a meaning. They simply expressed the fact that for Tom this was an important and exciting, a very special occasion.

The little girl took a step forward, caught her frock in both hands as if about to make a curtsy, rose upon her toes, and said in a prim voice, "I beg your pardon."

They both gazed at each other for some minutes with sparkling eyes. Neither smiled, but it seemed that both were about to smile.

Tom then gave another incomprehensible shout, ran round the table, sat down on the floor and began to play with a clockwork engine on a circular track. The little girl climbed on a tricycle and pedaled round the floor. "I can ride your bike," she said.

Tom paid no attention. He was trying how fast the engine could go without falling off the track.

The little girl took a picture book, sat down under the table with her back to Tom, and slowly, carefully, examined each page. "It's got a crooked wheel," Tom said, "that's what it is." The little girl made no answer. She was staring at the book with round eyes and a small pursed mouth—the expression of a nervous child at the zoo when the lions are just going to roar. Slowly and carefully she turned the next page. As it opened, her eyes became larger, her mouth more tightly pursed, as if she expected some creature to jump out at her.

"Tom." Nurse, having completed her private business, came bustling in with the air of one restored to life after a dangerous illness. "Tom, you naughty boy, is this the way you entertain your guests? Poor little Jenny, all by herself under the table." The nurse was plump and middle-aged; an old-fashioned nanny.

"She's not by herself," Tom said.

"Oh Tom, that really is naughty of you. Where are all your nice manners? Get up, my dear, and play with her like a good boy."

"I am playing with her," Tom said, in a surly tone, and he gave Nurse a sidelong glance of anger.

"Now Tom, if you go on telling such stories, I shall know you are trying to be naughty. Get up now when I ask you." She stooped, took Tom by the arm, and lifted him up. "Come now, you must be polite, after you've asked her yourself and pestered for her all the week."

At this public disclosure, Tom instantly lost his temper and yelled, "I didn't—I didn't—I won't—I won't."

"Then I'll have to take poor little Jenny downstairs again to her mummy."

"No—no—no."

"Will you play with her then?"

"No, I hate her—I never wanted her."

At this the little girl rose and said, in precise indignant tones, "He *is* naughty, isn't he?"

Tom flew at her, and seized her by the hair; the little girl at once uttered a loud scream, kicked him on the leg, and bit his arm. She was carried screaming to the door by Nurse, who, from there, issued sentence on

Tom, "I'm going straight to your father, as soon as he comes in." Then she went out, banging the door.

Tom ran at the door and kicked it, rushed at the engine, picked it up and flung it against the wall. Then he howled at the top of his voice for five minutes. He intended to howl all day. He was suffering from a large and complicated grievance.

All at once the door opened and the little girl walked in. She had an air of immense self-satisfaction as if she had just done something very clever. She said in a tone demanding congratulation. "I've come back."

Tom gazed at her through his tears and gave a loud sob. Then he picked up the engine, sat down by the track. But the engine fell off at the first push. He gave another sob, looked at the wheels, and bent one of them straight.

The little girl lifted her party frock behind in order not to crush it, sat down under the table, and drew the book onto her knee.

Tom tried the engine at high speed. His face was still set in the form of anger and bitterness, but he forgot to sob. He exclaimed with surprise and pleased excitement. "It's the lines too—where I trod on 'em."

The little girl did not reply. Slowly, carefully, she opened the book in the middle and gazed at an elephant. Her eyes became immense, her lips minute. But suddenly, and, as it were, accidentally, she gave an enormous sigh of relief, of happiness.

• 6 •

The Boy and the Watchman[1]

S. NELSON

WHEN I was six years old, I made a trip one cold winter night to a town about twenty miles away with my mother, another brother and sister, and my aunt and her little baby. The purpose of the trip was to go to a pharmacy to have a prescription filled for the baby which could not be obtained in the town we lived in. As we were returning, we were on a hill about seven miles from home when an axle broke. It was decided that I should walk to the nearest farm house, which was about half a mile away, and telephone my father so that he might come after us.

Being the oldest of the children, I went alone, because the ladies had to stay with the babies in the car. It was a very cold wintry night, the temperature was about twelve degrees below zero, and there was a strong wind. I was very frightened and very cold as I walked down the highway to the farmhouse. When I arrived

[1] Printed by permission.

there I found that there was no one home. In a way I was rather glad, because it gave me an excuse to hurry back to the car.

When I got back, the children were crying, and it was getting very cold. Something had to be done. Again it was decided that I should walk down the road, this time to a coal mine which was about one mile away. We were fairly sure that there was someone there all night long, so I started out again. I was very frightened and cold and I alternately ran and walked to the coal-mine. When I arrived at the engine-house, I could see that there was a light inside, and I could see the old watchman sitting by the fire. I pounded on the door quite a few times before he answered. He opened the inner door and left the outer storm door fastened. I told him what I wanted as best I could while trying to get my breath, explaining what had happened, who was in the car, where they were, that I wanted to use the phone to call my father. He slammed the door in my face and locked it and told me that no one could enter the building. I was frantic by this time and burst into tears, but he still refused to let me in, so I turned about and went back to the car. There still had been no passing vehicles and the children were getting cold and hungry.

This time it was decided that my mother and I would leave all three children with my aunt and walk to the nearest town which was about three miles away and telephone my father from there. As we came to the farmhouse that I had originally stopped at, we saw a light. Fortunately the farmer and his family had arrived home. We stopped, told him our difficulties and he very obligingly pulled us into the nearest town with his car. We telephoned my father who came to pick us up.

I didn't think too much about the incident the following day as I recall, but later on it came to mind and the more I thought about it the more angry I became, until I finally decided that, if I ever saw this man again, I would at least punch his nose for refusing to let me use the telephone that night. I carried this hatred on through the years, but fortunately, the old man died before I ever had occasion to meet him. It is a good thing that he did, because even in high school, when I was big enough to have done the job, I was still determined that I would if I saw him.

. . . . .

A few years ago, in conversation with a couple of friends of mine, the talk drifted around to this particular coal mine, and I related the story to my friends. One of them told me that he was very glad that I didn't ever get a chance to punch the old man's nose because that same old man had almost lost his life when he was beaten very badly by bandits who gained entrance to the building by asking permission to use the telephone.

• 7 •

Point of View[1]

A. AVERCHENKO

"MEN are comic!" she said, smiling dreamily. Not knowing whether this indicated praise or blame, I answered noncommittally: "Quite true."

"Really, my husband's a regular Othello. Sometimes I'm sorry I married him."

I looked helplessly at her. "Until you explain—" I began.

"Oh, I forgot that you haven't heard. About three weeks ago I was walking home with my husband through the square. I had a large black hat on, which suits me awfully well, and my cheeks were quite pink from walking. As we passed under a street light, a pale, dark-haired fellow standing near by glanced at me and suddenly took my husband by his sleeve.

" 'Would you oblige me with a light?' he says. Alexander pulled his arm away, stooped down, and quicker

[1] *This Week Magazine*, August 16, 1947, p. 2. Reprinted by permission.

than lightning banged him on the head with a brick. He fell like a log. Awful."

"Why, what on earth made your husband get jealous all of a sudden?"

She shrugged her shoulders. "I told you men are very comic."

Bidding her farewell, I went out, and at the corner came across her husband.

"Hello, old chap," I said. "They tell me you've been breaking people's heads."

He burst out laughing. "So you've been talking to my wife. It was jolly lucky that brick came so pat into my hand. Otherwise, just think: I had about fifteen hundred rubles in my pocket, and my wife was wearing her diamond earrings."

"Do you think he wanted to rob you?"

"A man accosts you in a deserted spot, asks for a light and gets hold of your arm. What more do you want?"

Perplexed, I left him and walked on.

"There's no catching you today," I heard a voice say from behind.

I looked around and saw a friend I hadn't set eyes upon for three weeks.

"Lord!" I exclaimed. "What on earth has happened to you?"

He smiled faintly and asked in turn: "Do you know whether any lunatics have been at large lately? I was attacked by one three weeks ago. I left the hospital only today."

With sudden interest, I asked: "Three weeks ago! Were you sitting in the square?"

"Yes, I was. The most absurd thing. I was sitting in the square dying for a smoke. No matches! After ten minutes or so, a gentleman passes with some old hag. He was smoking. I go up to him, touch him on the sleeve and ask in my most polite manner: 'Can you oblige me with a light?' And what d'you think? The madman stoops down, picks something up, and the next moment I am lying on the ground with a broken head, unconscious. You probably read about it in the newspaper."

I looked at him, and asked earnestly: "Do you really believe you met up with a lunatic?"

"I am sure of it."

An hour afterwards I was eagerly digging in old back numbers of the local paper. At last I found what I was looking for: a short note in the accident column:

UNDER THE INFLUENCE OF DRINK

Yesterday morning, the keepers of the square found on a bench a young man whose papers show him to be of good family. He had evidently fallen to the ground while in a state of extreme intoxication, and had broken his head on a nearby brick. The distress of this prodigal's parents is indescribable.

PART II

The office of the scholar is to cheer, to raise, to guide men by showing them facts amidst appearances.

—Ralph Waldo Emerson

• 8 •

On the Use of Language[1]

OLIVER GOLDSMITH

THE manner in which most writers begin their treatises on the use of language is generally thus:—"Language has been granted to man, in order to discover his wants and necessities, so as to have them relieved by society. Whatever we desire, whatever we wish, it is but to clothe those desires or wishes in words, in order to fruition. The principal use of language, therefore," say they, "is to express our wants, so as to receive a speedy redress."

Such an account as this may serve to satisfy grammarians and rhetoricians well enough, but men who know the world maintain very contrary maxims; they hold, and I think with some show of reason, that he who best knows how to conceal his necessity and desires is the most likely person to find redress, and that the true use of speech is not so much to express our wants, as to conceal them.

[1] *The Bee,* No. III, Oct. 20, 1759.

When we reflect on the manner in which mankind generally confer their favours, we shall find that they who seem to want them least are the very persons who most liberally share them. There is something so attractive in riches, that the large heap generally collects from the smaller; and the poor find as much pleasure in increasing the enormous mass, as the miser who owns it sees happiness in its increase. Nor is there in this anything repugnant to the laws of true morality. Seneca himself allows that, in conferring benefits, the present should always be suited to the dignity of the receiver. Thus the rich receive large presents, and are thanked for accepting them; men of middling stations are obliged to be content with presents something less; while the beggar, who may be truly said to want indeed, is well paid if a farthing rewards his warmest solicitations.

Every man who has seen the world, and has had his ups and downs in life, as the expression is, must have frequently experienced the truth of this doctrine, and must know, that to have much, or to seem to have it, is the only way to have more. Ovid finely compares a man of broken fortune to a falling column; the lower it sinks, the greater weight it is obliged to sustain. Thus, when a man has no occasion to borrow, he finds numbers willing to lend him. Should he ask his friend to lend him a hundred pounds, it is possible, from the largeness of his demand, he may find credit for twenty; but should he humbly only sue for a trifle, it is two to one whether he might be trusted for two-pence. A certain young fellow at George's, whenever he had occasion to ask his friend for a guinea, used to prelude his request as if he wanted two hundred, and talked so familiarly of large sums, that none could ever think he wanted a small one. The same gentleman, whenever he wanted credit for a new suit from his tailor, always made a proposal in laced clothes: for he found by experience that if he appeared shabby on these occasions, Mr. Lynch had taken an oath against trusting; or, what was every bit as bad, his foreman was out of the way, and would not be at home these two days.

There can be no inducement to reveal our wants, except to find pity, and by this means relief; but before a poor man opens his mind in such circumstances, he should first consider whether he is contented to lose the esteem of the person he solicits, and whether he is willing to give up friendship only to excite compassion. Pity and friendship are passions incompatible with each other, and it is impossible that both can reside in any breast for the smallest space, without impairing each other. Friendship is made up of esteem and pleasure; pity is composed of sorrow and contempt: the mind may for some time fluctuate between them, but it never can entertain both together.

Yet let it not be thought that I would exclude pity from the human mind. There are scarcely any who are not, in some degree, possessed of this pleasing softness; but it is at best but a short-lived passion, and seldom affords distress more than transitory assistance: with some it scarcely lasts from the first impulse till the hand can be put into the pocket; with others it may continue for twice that space, and on some of extraordinary sensibility I have seen it operate for half an hour. But, however, last as it will, it generally produces but beggarly effects; and where, from this motive, we give a halfpenny, from others we give always pounds. In great distress we sometimes, it is true, feel the influence of tenderness strongly; when the same distress solicits a second time, we then feel with diminished sensibility; but, like the repetition of an echo, every new impulse becomes weaker, till at last our sensations lose every mixture of sorrow, and degenerate into downright contempt.

Jack Spindle and I were old acquaintance; but he's gone. Jack was bred in a compting-house, and his father, dying just as he was out of his time, left him a handsome fortune, and many friends to advise with. The restraint in which he had been brought up had thrown a gloom upon his temper, which some regarded as habitual prudence, and from such considerations he had every day repeated offers of friendship. Those who had money were ready to offer him their assistance that way; and they who had daughters frequently, in the warmth of affection, advised him to marry. Jack, however, was in good circumstances; he wanted neither money, friends, nor a wife, and therefore modestly declined their proposals.

Some errors in the management of his affairs and several losses in trade soon brought Jack to a different way of thinking; and he at last thought it his best way to let his friends know, that their offers were at length acceptable. His first address was, therefore, to a scrivener who had formerly made him frequent offers of money and friendship at a time when, perhaps, he knew those offers would have been refused.

Jack, therefore, thought he might use his old friend without any ceremony; and, as a man confident of not being refused, requested the use of an hundred guineas for a few days, as he just them had an occasion for money. "And pray, Mr. Spindle," replied the scrivener, "do you want all this money?"—"Want it, sir," says the other; "if I did not want it, I should not have asked it." —"I am sorry for that," says the friend; "for those who want money when they come to borrow, will want money when they should come to pay. To say the truth, Mr. Spindle, money is money now-a-days. I believe it is all sunk in the bottom of the sea, for my part; and he that has got a little is a fool if he does not keep what he has got."

Not quite disconcerted by this refusal, our adventurer was resolved to apply to another, whom he knew to be the very best friend he had in the world. The gentleman whom he now addressed received his proposal with all the affability that could be expected from generous friendship. "Let me see,—you want an hundred guineas; and pray, dear Jack, would not fifty answer?"—"If you have but fifty to spare, sir, I must be contented." —"Fifty to spare! I do not say that, for I believe I have but twenty about me."—"Then I must borrow the other thirty from some other friend."—"And pray," replied the friend, "would it not be the best way to borrow the whole money from that other friend? then one note will serve for all, you know? Lord, Mr. Spindle, make no ceremony with me at any time; you know I'm your friend, when you choose a bit of dinner or so. You, Tom, see the gentleman down. You won't forget to dine with us now and then? Your very humble servant."

Distressed, but not discouraged at this treatment, he was at last resolved to find that assistance from love which he could not have from friendship. Miss Jenny Dismal had a fortune in her own hands, and she had already made all the advances that her sex's modesty would permit. He made his proposal, therefore, with confidence, but soon perceived "No bankrupt ever found the fair one kind." Miss Jenny and Master Billy Galoon were lately fallen deeply in love with each other, and the whole neighbourhood thought it would soon be a match.

Every day now began to strip Jack of his former finery; his clothes flew piece by piece to the pawnbrokers; and he seemed at length equipped in the genuine mourning of antiquity. But still he thought himself secure from starving; the numberless invitations he had received to dine, even after his losses, were yet unanswered: he was, therefore, now resolved to accept of a dinner, because he wanted one; and in this manner he actually lived among his friends a whole week without being openly affronted. The last place I saw poor Jack was at the Reverend Dr. Gosling's. He had, as he fancied, just nicked the time, for he came in just as the cloth was laying. He took a chair without being desired, and talked for some time without being attended to. He assured the company, that nothing procured so good an appetite as a walk to White Conduit House, where he had been that morning. He looked at the tablecloth, and praised the figure of the damask; talked of a feast where he had been the day before, but that the venison was overdone. All this, however, procured the poor creature no invitation, and he was not yet sufficiently hardened to stay without being asked; wherefore, finding the gentleman of the house insensible to all his fetches, he thought proper at last to retire, and mend his appetite by a walk in the Park.

You then, O ye beggars of my acquaintance, whether in rags or lace—whether in Kent Street or the Mall—whether at Smyrna or St. Giles's—might I advise you as a friend, never seem in what of the favour which you solicit. Apply to every passion but pity for redress. You may find relief from vanity, from self-interest, or from avarice, but seldom from compassion. The very eloquence of a poor man is disgusting; and that mouth which is opened, even for flattery, is seldom expected to close without a petition.

If, then, you would ward off the gripe of poverty, pretend to be a stranger to her, and she will at least use you with a ceremoney. Hear not my advice, but that of Ofellus. If you be caught dining upon a halfpenny porringer of pease soup and potatoes, praise the wholesomeness of your frugal repast. You may observe that Dr. Cheyne has prescribed pease broth for the gravel; hint that you are not one of those who are always making a god of your belly. If you are obliged to wear a flimsy stuff in the midst of winter, be the first to remark that stuffs are very much worn at Paris. If there be found some irreparable defects in any part of your equipage, which cannot be concealed by all the arts of sitting cross-legged, coaxing, or darning, say that neither you nor Sampson Gideon were ever very fond of dress. Or if you be a philosopher, hint that Plato and Seneca are the tailors you choose to employ; assure the company, that men ought to be content with a bare covering, since what is now so much the pride of some, was formerly our shame. Horace will give you a Latin sentence fit for the occasion,—

Toga defendere frigus,
Quamvis crassa, queat.

In short, however caught, do not give up, but ascribe to the frugality of your disposition what others might be apt to attribute to the narrowness of your circumstances, and appear rather to be a miser than a beggar. To be poor, and to seem poor, is a certain method never to rise. Pride in the great is hateful, in the wise it is ridiculous; beggarly pride is the only sort of vanity I can excuse.

• 9 •

"Get off Route 25, Young Man"[1]

CHARLES F. KETTERING

MY HOME is in Dayton, Ohio, and I was a friend of the Wright family and learned to fly on the very early Wright airplanes. Their first flight was on the 17th of December, 46 years ago. Everyone was perfectly sure that it was a crazy thing to try. The undertakers moved into Kitty Hawk with a number of caskets because they thought the Wrights would kill themselves.

When they made those first three flights on December 17, 1903, they wired their sister that they had succeeded, that they were very happy, and that they should be home for Christmas.

She thought it was a world-shaking event, so she very excitedly called a Dayton newspaper on the telephone. She rang and rang and rang. The newspaper boys were playing pinochle, but finally one of them answered.

He said, "Yes?"

[1] From the article with that title in *Collier's*, Dec. 3, 1949, pp. 13–14. Reprinted by permission.

She said, "This is Katherine Wright speaking," and very excitedly read the telegram.

He said, "Good. Glad to hear the boys are going to get home for Christmas," and hung up the telephone.

The newspaperman said to the others: "Nobody's going to catch me on that, because it has been proved mathematically that a heavier-than-air machine can't fly."

An inventor often has to overcome so-called "proof" or his own work may be perfectly useless.

I had a friend who was the research and development man for one of the British railroads. He came to this country to deliver a commencement address at a technical university. After the address he came to Detroit to see our laboratories.

"Ket," he said, "when you were over in London last year you told me some things you fellows were doing with Diesel locomotives and you lied to me."

I said, "Not intentionally."

"But," he said, "you told me you were running these locomotives about a hundred miles an hour."

I said, "We are."

"And that you were taking power on the front wheels; that is, the wheels that are ahead."

I said, "We are."

He said, "I have the formulas in my portfolio that say you can't do that."

I said, "For Heaven's sake, don't let the locomotive know about it."

I said to him, "I won't argue with you at all." I took the telephone, called Chicago and got him transportation from Chicago to Denver, and flew him to Chicago to make the connection. He made the trip to Denver, where I had him ride part way on the Diesel engines.

He stopped in to see me on his way back. He was returning to England. I said, "I didn't expect to see you again. Did you ride that locomotive?"

"Yes," he said.

"Did it go a hundred miles an hour?"

"It did."

"Well," I said, "that's the reason I didn't expect to see you back. Maybe you forgot to take the portfolio with the equations in it."

He said, "The thing that amazes me is why we could be so one hundred per cent wrong."

I said, "You weren't wrong. You didn't start in right."

The two of us got out his formulas. He wasn't talking about our locomotive at all. Our locomotive uses an ordinary truck like a streetcar's. He was talking about a locomotive with a rigid frame which would normally have a small-wheel lead truck in front of it.

I said, "What's the use of using mathematics on one kind of thing and then applying it to another which is in no way related? It isn't even a second cousin to it."

We sometimes set up these limiting conditions, and they keep us from trying out experiments.

The Inventor Tries His Product

One of the great differences between the inventor and other men is that he is willing to try the thing. In the airplane experiment, the Wright Brothers had first flown kites and had drawn knowledge from them. They finally said, "If we had an engine we could fly," and kept trying and trying until they did fly with an engine they were forced to develop themselves. They didn't care what anybody thought about it; they were pretty sure they could do it because the birds were flying.

The inventor, in addition to having to forecast what he thinks can be done, has to overcome commercial opposition to the idea.

When we first put self-starters on automobiles I attended a meeting of the American Institute of Electrical Engineers. They asked me if I would make a little talk on the self-starter, and I did.

One fellow got up and said, "No wonder you made your self-starter work; you profaned every law of electrical engineering."

I didn't profane any fundamental laws of electrical engineering. All I did was make the starter work. Those laws had nothing whatever to do with self-starters; they were written for something entirely different.

There are fundamentals in inventions, engineering and development that are true in everything else.

As I said before, my home is in Dayton, and we have had our laboratories for years in Detroit, which is several hundred miles away. I keep my home in Ohio and drive back and forth week ends.

Some of the people who work with me also drive between Dayton and Detroit. One said, "I understand you drive from here to Dayton in four and one-half hours."

I said, "I can do that once in a while, depending on traffic."

He said, "I don't believe it."

I said, "But I do it."

He said, "I'm a much better driver than you are, and I can't do it."

I said, "I'm going down Friday. Why don't you ride along with me?"

So we rode into Dayton in about four and one-half hours, or a little more, and he said, "Hell, no wonder you can do it. You didn't stay on Route 25!"

Now, Route 25 is the red line that is marked on all the maps between Detroit and Dayton. If you are a stranger, that's the road you should take. It never occurred to my colleague that you could take any other road on either side of Route 25. There's a lot of country on either side of it; in fact, half the earth is on each side of it.

Often the biggest problem the inventor has is not in getting his apparatus to work, but in getting it to work in tune with what the public thinks at the time.

• 10 •

Barriers to Understanding Between Officers and Enlisted Men[1]

SAMUEL A. STOUFFER, ET AL.

ALTHOUGH the Army's social system was such that officers with the best will in the world would find it difficult to bridge the gulf which separated them from the thoughts and feelings of the men under their command, one of the surprises experienced by the observant social scientist in the Army was the number of officers who assumed, apparently quite sincerely, that they succeeded in so doing.

All comparative studies made by the Research Branch showed that officers tended to believe that their men were more favorably disposed on any given point than the men's own anonymous responses showed the men to be.

[1] Reprinted from Samuel A. Stouffer, Edward A. Suchman, Leland C. DeVinney, Shirley A. Star, and Robin M. Williams, Jr., *The American Soldier*, Vol. I: Adjustment During Army Life, pp. 391–395, by permission of the authors and the publisher. Copyright, 1949, by the Princeton University Press.

Table 1 presents a typical illustration of this wishful thinking on the part of officers. In each of 53 Infantry rifle companies in the United States, the company commander was asked a question like the following:

How many of your enlisted men would you say feel proud of their company?

______Almost none of them
______About one fourth of them
______About half of them
______About three fourths of them
______Almost all of them

TABLE 1. Accuracy of Estimates by Company Commanders of Favorable Attitudes Among Men in Their Own Company

Attitude Area	Number of Companies in Which the CO: Over-estimated	Estimated Correctly	Under-estimated	Total
Pride in outfit	43	8	2	53
Desire to be a soldier	42	4	7	53
Satisfaction with job	33	18	2	53
Importance of Infantry	31	14	8	53

Data from S-121, United States, April 1944.

The men in the same company were asked:

Do you feel proud of your company?

______Yes, very proud
______Yes, fairly proud
______No, not proud
______Undecided

If over 87½ per cent of the men checked either "very proud" or "fairly proud," the CO was considered correct if his answer was "almost all of the men" would say they felt proud of their company. If 62½ to 87½ per cent of the men checked "very proud" or "fairly proud," the CO was considered correct if he checked "about three fourths." Enlisted checks by 37½ to 62½ per cent were equated with officers' checks of "about half"; enlisted checks by 12½ to 37½ per cent of the unit sample were equated with officers' checks of "about a fourth," and enlisted checks by less than 12½ per cent with officers' checks of "almost none."

As Table 1 shows, 8 of the 53 officers estimated their men's responses correctly by the above definition. But 43 *overestimated* the proportion of their men who would say they were proud of their company, as contrasted with only 2 who *underestimated*. The same tendency is seen with respect to other items shown in Table 1.[2]

The same tendency was observed in studies overseas as well as in the United States.

Psychologically, one of the elements in this habit of officers of overestimating their men's favorable attitudes

[2] These items were:

"If it were up to you to choose, do you think you could do more for your country as a soldier or as a worker in a war job?" (As a soldier, as a war worker, undecided.)

"How satisfied are you about being in your present Army job instead of some other Army job?" (Very satisfied, satisfied, makes no difference, dissatisfied, very dissatisfied.)

"How important a part do you think the Infantry will play in winning the war?" (A very important part, a fairly important part, not a very important part, not important at all.)

was a product of the tendency to project one's own attitudes upon the men. Overseas studies of officers and men who were veterans of Infantry campaigns showed that if officers felt in rather low spirits they tended to think that enlisted men did also, while if the officers manifested high spirits they tended to think enlisted men did the same. How much this represents projection only and how much, if at all, it represents some possible causal connection (e.g., if officers have low spirits this will infect the men) or some other association (e.g., officers and the men they know best have shared very similar experiences), cannot be separately determined from the data.

In so far as the tendency to projection existed, the net effect ordinarily would be to lead officers to overestimate the favorableness of men's attitudes—for the reason that officers' own attitudes generally were more favorable than the men's.

Characteristic differences in attitudes between officers and enlisted men are evident in almost any area one could mention. With very few exceptions, officers tended to have more favorable attitudes toward all aspects of the military system than enlisted men. They were more content with Army life; they were more satisfied with their jobs; they had greater pride in being soldiers; they had less aggression against the Army, and so on through the whole gamut of attitudes toward the structure and functioning of military society.

In Table 2 are presented some of these comparisons in attitudes drawn from scattered studies in which, in each case, cross sections of officers and enlisted men in

Table 2. Comparison of Officers' and Enlisted Men's Attitudes on Selected Subjects

	Officers	Enlisted Men
Question: "How interested are you in the work you are doing in your present Army assignment?"[a]		
Per cent saying, "Very much interested"	82	50
Question: "In general do you feel that you yourself have gotten a square deal from the Army?"[a]		
Per cent saying, "Yes, in most ways I have"	65	41
Question: "In general, how would you say you feel most of the time, in good spirits or in low spirits?"[b]		
Per cent saying, "I am usually in good spirits"	53	24
Question: "What do you think of military control and discipline at this post?"[b]		
Per cent saying, "It's about right"	62	42
Question: "How many of your officers are the kind who are willing to go through anything they ask their men to go through?"[c]		
Per cent saying, "All" or "Most"	92	37
Question: (On the whole do you agree or disagree with the statement) "The Army would be a lot better if officers and enlisted men were more friendly with each other"[d]		
Per cent saying, "Disagree"	47	15

[a] Cross section of 5,000 officers and 3,500 enlisted men in the

the same units were asked parallel questions. In no case can the observed differences in response be accounted for simply in terms of differences in background characteristics. It is difficult to account for such differences in attitudes except in terms of a class patterning of views.

Apparent class differences in thinking between officers and enlisted men extend, as has been indicated, to many different areas. It is interesting, however, to note one bit of evidence that these differences appear to be sharpest on matters which tend to reflect on those aspects of the military system which place the enlisted class at a disadvantage relative to the officer class and for which officers are likely to feel some responsibility. In the February 1945 survey of 5,000 officers and 3,500 enlisted men in the United States, cited in Table 2, the following question was asked: "Below is a list of things enlisted men commonly gripe about. In your experience which of these do you think enlisted men usually have good reasons to gripe about?" Table 3 shows the percentages of officers and men who said they think enlisted men usually have good reason to gripe about each item. It will be noted that the first four gripes on the list, where the differences in attitudes are the sharpest, all relate to matters in which enlisted men are disad-

---

United States surveyed in February 1945. (S-198-O and E.)

[b] Cross section of 595 officers and 808 enlisted men in the India-Burma Theater surveyed in July 1945. (S-219 and 220.)

[c] Cross section of 444 officers and 4,078 enlisted men in two Infantry divisions in the South Pacific Theater surveyed in March 1944. (S-124.)

[d] Cross section of 323 officers and 954 enlisted men in the United States surveyed in November 1945. (S-234B.)

vantaged relative to officers and for which officers are likely to feel some direct responsibility. The last two gripes on the list, concerning which there are practically no differences in attitude between officers and men, are matters for which officers are less likely to feel responsible and from which they are likely to feel they themselves suffer almost as much as enlisted men.

From the same study on which Table 3 is based comes an exemplification of the point illustrated earlier, in Table 1, of the tendency for officers to overestimate the favorableness and underestimate the unfavorableness of enlisted men's responses. Both officers and men were asked to check the following statement: "Most enlisted men do *not* respect their officers.—Agree—Disagree." Only 25 per cent of the officers agreed, as contrasted with 54 per cent of the enlisted men.

While psychological interpretations in terms of projection will help explain the discrepancy between what officers thought men felt and what the men felt, it must be recognized that the basic social system of the Army impeded rather than facilitated a meeting of minds. Not only were the experiences of officers and men different, but also the barriers of power and social distance were almost insurmountable.

The power relationship was an obvious barrier. A considerable difference in perspective between officers who exercise authority and men over whom the authority is exercised is probably inevitable, at least in an organization operated on an authoritarian basis. And whether in the Army or elsewhere, completely candid interchange of attitudes on all subjects does not ordinarily occur between those who wield power and those who are subject to that power.

But in the Army this inescapable barrier was augmented by the fostering of status differences and physical as well as social distance between officers and men. Officers could be easily misled by the rituals of deference exacted from all enlisted men. They were "sirred" and saluted and rarely answered back. It is easy to understand how during the course of time they could come to mistake these compulsory outward symbols of deference for voluntary respect and fail to perceive underlying hostilities and resentments. Officers were practically entrapped into assuming that they were symbols of respected authority.

It is easy to understand, too, how the different treatment accorded to officers because of their different status blurred their insight into some typical enlisted attitudes and the reasons for those attitudes. Some flavor of the status difference between officers and enlisted men and of one type of difference in treatment that went with it is revealed in the following account written for the Research Branch by an officer commissioned directly from the ranks. The actual episode may have been an unusual one, but it is illustrative of some common underlying attitudes:

After being commissioned and discharged as an enlisted man I was transferred to station complement to be sent from camp. I had to check over some items of clothing with the supply sergeant of the new assignment. Not wishing to put on my uniform until I was ready to go, I was wearing the clothes of a private. As I stepped into the supply room

TABLE 3. Comparison of Officers' and Enlisted Men's Attitudes Toward Enlisted Men's Complaints[a]

	Per Cent Who Think Enlisted Men "Usually Have Good Reason to Gripe" About Listed Complaint		
	Among Enlisted Men (N = 2377)	Among Officers (N = 5000)	Difference
"Discipline too strict about petty things"	51	23	28
"Not enough passes and furloughs"	53	28	25
"The wrong men get the breaks"	53	28	25
"Too much 'chicken' to put up with"	71	49	22
"Work too hard or hours too long	23	9	14
"Too much time wasted during the day"[b]	48	59	−11
"Wrong job assignment"	64	59	5
"Promotions frozen or too slow"	69	68	1

Data from S-198-O, EA and EB, United States, February 1945.

[a] The question asked was, "Below is a list of things enlisted men commonly gripe about. In your experience which of these do you think enlisted men usually have good reasons to gripe about?"

[b] It is possible that officers and men interpreted this item differently. Enlisted men commonly gripe about their time being wasted by officers requiring them to wait, a complaint epitomized in the Army expression, "Hurry up and wait." Officers, on the other hand, are more likely to be critical of time wasted by enlisted men through goldbricking and dilatory tactics.

the Sergeant was not there, but a few privates were waiting. Being in a hurry I started to look for him in the next room. Just as he came into the room, leaving me and a couple of other privates a little ways in the supply room, his opening remark, with a belligerent glare, was: "How about over there behind that counter" and without waiting for compliance, "and what's the matter with you getting out of there too," was directed at me, I being a little further in the room than the other two. I moved out and said nothing.

The first man to the desk was handing in laundry. The Sergeant took the slip. "God damn, this isn't the way to make out a laundry slip. Haven't you been shown how to make this out right?" The man said "no." "Yes you have, by God and don't tell me you haven't. Weren't you in that formation yesterday? Yes, I thought so. I told every one of you how to do this right. By Jesus, you haven't any more brains than a frog on a railroad track. Now you take that slip and you make it out right." Here was the noncom in perfect form and attitude. He turned to me next. "Now what the hell do you want?" It was a little extra strong. He remembered I had gotten in his way a moment before. I wanted to see what would happen so I quietly told him that I had been commissioned an officer and transferred prior to leaving camp and that I'd like to check some clothes off. "Oh yes sir, I'll take care of that right now." He was all courtesy and service. He wanted to fix things about himself and ended up with an apology for treating me as he had, saying "I certainly wouldn't have if I'd known." The fact is that he hadn't been out of form at all. I just occupied two roles which brought out the contrast sharply.[3]

[3] By William Reeder.

• 11 •

Refresher Course[1]

ETHEL H. GERSTIN

"I JUST did something awfully stupid," we blithely announce. There is almost a note of pride in our voices because in our hearts we feel that no one who knows us could believe us capable of something really stupid. Yet that note of indulgence for our own stupidity is oddly lacking when we say (and who among us hasn't?), "I just don't understand how they can possibly be so stupid!" referring of course to our students. How often we become exasperated and self-righteously indignant. We worked so hard; we explained everything so clearly; we went over it several times; the material was so simple! They seemed to understand; yet the results showed they didn't. How *could* they be so stupid?

I Take a Course

A recent personal experience unexpectedly answered this usually rhetorical question for me and made me a

[1] From *High Points*, January 1952, pp. 10–12. Reprinted by permission.

little more sympathetic and understanding. Having bought a sewing machine, I decided I ought to learn how to sew and promptly registered for a sewing course. Dutifully I selected a pattern and set out to follow it, only to find myself completely baffled by a situation I had not been confronted with before. Here before me were simple words forming simple directions; yet they conveyed nothing to me. I was highly chagrined. After all, I had been reading all my life, following instructions, solving problems; yet these "simple" directions, followed so casually and intelligently by thousands of women *without* college degrees, were gibberish to me. I could minimize the blow to my pride by explaining to myself that naturally I wouldn't immediately understand something for which I had no background and whose vocabulary was incomprehensible to me. But how rightfully the instructor might have said to me, "I don't see how anyone could possibly be so stupid: The instructions were so clear!" And the fifteen-year-old girl in the course (who happened to be a student in my own school) could have echoed her. Perhaps *she* could not understand too readily the *Odyssey* and *Silas Marner* or the intricacies of grammatical constructions, but the instructions on a sewing pattern presented no difficulties to her.

And I'm Humbled

Other experiences in this sewing course made me realize anew something I had evidently been losing sight of—how involved the learning process really is. Whenever the instructor explained or demonstrated something, I listened and watched very attentively. I was sure I understood and would know exactly how to do it by myself—was sure, that is, until I reached home and tried it. At the next session I took notes and drew diagrams but even then found that I floundered. "Memory is certainly a fickle thing," I forgave myself jauntily. "I suppose it just takes several explanations and more practice to make things stick."

With a sense of guilt I recalled that I had not been quite so forgiving to many students who had come to me at times and said, "I didn't do my homework last night because I didn't understand it," adding in answer to my skeptical look and remark that probably they hadn't paid too close attention in class, "Honest, I was sure I understood it when I left class yesterday." My own recent learning problems in an unfamiliar field made me accept for the first time that most of them had really been telling the truth and not malingering at all. It was a humbling and beneficial experience. If I could not grasp easily something as specific as sewing, why should I have been so aghast when young people, who usually dealt in specifics, could not cope with abstractions as readily as I thought they should? The experiences and language needed to understand the abstract ideas and concepts encountered in literature, in grammar, in mathematics, etc., were as foreign to them as the sewing vocabulary had been to me.

Most of our students are certainly not stupid. Can it be that, all too frequently, we use this term to express our opinion of them because we have become impatient with the learning process? Can it be that we tend to forget that only time, patience, experience, and constant practice will eventually give students the tools they need for comprehension and remembering?

Moral for Alertness Courses

After one has taught for a number of years, it becomes increasingly difficult to be patient with the slowness and seeming stupidity of others. For that reason I feel that the Board of Education is making a serious mistake in insisting that teachers take courses in their own specialized fields. When we take such courses, we encounter no learning difficulties, nothing to jolt us out of our smugness. I think the Board of Education should permit, if not insist on, a certain number of courses in areas completely unrelated to our specialties. Perhaps we need our egos deflated occasionally by being made to struggle with something *unfamiliar* so that, as teachers, we can keep the complexities of the learning process fresh before us. Then maybe we will allow the same indulgence for our students' "Stupidity" as we do for our own.

• 12 •

Teaching Fenestration Surgery[1]

SAMUEL ROSEN, M.D.

From 1938 to 1948 about 500 of our best otologists from every part of the country and a few from other lands attempted to learn the fenestration operation. Less than 100 of these men who took the prescribed course are now doing fenestration surgery adequately. The purpose of this article is to indicate one of the important reasons for the failure of many to continue to do fenestration surgery after completing the prescribed course in spite of the financial sacrifice involved in training (cost of transportation, loss of income from practice, tuition fee, instruments, and living expenses estimated at about five to ten thousand dollars.)

During the six-week course the student watches experts perform about forty fenestration operations on the living. At the same time each student performs

[1] From the Otolaryngological Service, The Mount Sinai Hospital, New York, N.Y. Editorial, *The American Journal of Surgery*, Vol. LXXX, pp. 491–492. Reprinted by permission of the author and editor.

about fifteen operations on the cadaver. Both teacher and student assume that the conclusion of the six-week course will find each student equipped to perform this most difficult of all surgical procedures. The facts invalidate this assumption.

Why does this misevaluation persist? In the earliest days of the fenestration operation the teacher must have predicted that just such a six-week course would train each student to perform the operation on the living adequately. The student expected and hoped that this prediction would be accurate. However, too many men found at the end of the course that their individual performance on patients was not sufficiently successful for them to continue in this work. Since the performance of these surgeons was not up to their expectations, they believed the entire reason for their failure lay within themselves—that unless they could perform the operation with absolute success they were "absolute" failures. They therefore ceased doing the operation. Thus for years a mutual misevaluation of the course by both teacher and student ensued which has perpetuated much trained incapacity.

Actually there are only degrees of success in performance. The degree of skill acquired in this operation is in direct proportion to the degree of practice on the cadaver. This would apply to learning almost any technical skill. Therefore, the six-week course should be regarded as the first phase of learning the fenestration operation, to be followed with repetitive cadaver operations until expert skill has been achieved. If this simple truth had been applied, almost every one of the 400 nonperforming otologists would now be doing fenestration surgery. This is not to imply that adequate cadaver practice would result in equal skill for all, but it would result in more adequate performance. At the end of the six-week course the basic evaluation of the student should not be, "I am a failure because I cannot perform the operation with absolute success," but rather, "Further practice on the cadaver will develop my skill to that of an expert." One must repeat over and over this complicated technic on all sorts of variable anatomic specimens so that final performance will be highly skilful and fluent.[2]

As the student watches the expert operate with ease and smoothness, he observes perfection; but seldom does the student benefit by witnessing errors in technic, even on the cadaver. Too little of the dangers of the operation are demonstrated. Errors as well as perfect technic should be thoroughly learned on the cadaver.

Students doing cadaver work in a class unwittingly compete with each other. When a student makes a vital technical blunder which others in the class avoided, he tends to make a poor evaluation of himself, with resulting tension. This tension increases the tendency to blunder. It is recommended, therefore, that after completing the course the student perform the rest of his cadaver operations alone and in silence. In such a relaxing atmosphere learning becomes amazingly rapid.

The formal course in fenestration surgery should explicitly denote that at the end of six weeks the student

[2] Rosen, Samuel. Learning the Lempert fenestration operation. *Arch. Otolaryng.*, 45: 335–338, 1947.

is, as a rule, not yet ready for the operating room but must continue the cadaver work at his leisure until he becomes expert. A well trained otologist wishing to learn this operation need not necessarily take a formal course provided he can observe expert surgeons operate and then perform about 100 cadaver operations himself.

The principle of practice makes perfect is simple and some will feel offended that such an obvious principle should be so stressed. Yet objective analysis would indicate that no matter how much this simple principle is approved verbally, in most cases it is not fully applied in practice.

The six-week course of fenestration surgery is excellent as a beginning. The completion of the course should then become the signal for much more cadaver practice until perfection is achieved. Most of the surgeons who discontinued the fenestration operation could and should rehabilitate themselves by resuming cadaver practice.

• 13 •

Man, Dig These Crazy Tests! (To Evaluate Advertising Copy)[1]

JOHN S. COOPER

THE clever psychologists who mastermind the efforts to sell you such things as toothpaste, cigarets, deodorants, and beer are beginning to resort to methods formerly tried only on disturbed mental patients.

The Szondi test, doll playing, Rorschach ink blots, thematic apperception, Rozenzweig picture frustration, and other esoteric testing schemes borrowed from mental institutions are being used increasingly every day to find out things about you that you don't even know yourself.

Especially devised to penetrate the public subconscious, these devices ferret out the hidden prejudices and yearnings that wouldn't show up in an ordinary question-and-answer marketing poll. In psychologists'

[1] A story datelined Chicago in *The Wall Street Journal*, Dec. 29, 1952, pp. 1, 9. Reprinted by permission.

jargon they are "projective techniques," and they are getting special attention at the current midwinter convention of the American Marketing Association.

"Projectives can catch the personality with its guard down," one marketing expert explains. They are being used in testing advertising copy, naming new products and devising slogans. They are especially valuable in marketing products used on private parts of the body or with sexual connotations or on products involving an individual's social position and prestige.

The field is so new there aren't even any textbooks on the subject. But James M. Vicary, a New York research consultant, estimates that already about two dozen marketing organizations have begun to use projectives.

Conservative institutions such as the *Chicago Tribune* and Commonwealth Edison Co. have resorted to them. Government agencies have been dabbling with them. And in an election prediction poll in Philadelphia, Erasmo Bucci used psychiatric methods to sweat out his "undecided" vote, ending up with a prediction on the election of Gov. Fine within one percentage point of the final result.

"These approaches will become increasingly important in market research in the future," says Harold J. Leavitt, vice president of Nejelski & Co., management counsel of New York.

Word Association

So far, word association has been the most common psychiatric device used by market researchers to probe the public mind. By asking human "guinea pigs" to respond to a list of words with the first word that comes to their minds, like "bread"—"butter"; "C.I.O."—"union," or "detergent"—"soap,"—a surprising amount can be learned about the hidden emotional tags that words carry.

Take the case of the brewer who wanted to use the coined word "lagered" to describe his beer in advertising. In a word association test, only 35% of the people gave associations like "beer," "ale," or "stout." Another 38% gave such responses as "slow," "tired," "drunk," "behind," "linger," and "dizzy" and the remaining 26% had no response at all. P.S.—"Lagered" was thrown out.

Commonwealth Edison wanted to find out what themes and descriptive words could be used in ads to attract new industry to Chicago. The stimulus word "Chicago" means many things to many people but, in word association tests, most of them thought in terms of agriculture and, secondly, industry. The resulting ad, carefully worded and captioned "agriculture and industry are partners in Chicago and northern Illinois" brought a record number of inquiries.

Coined words are a big factor in advertising. Specially cooked up gems like "irium," "seismotite," "activated," "chlorophylin," "acetaniled," "silicone," "sanforized," "cravenette," and "solium" all have been through the word association mill before they were sprung on the unsuspecting public.

Psychologist Vicary even used this method to name his children. "My wife and I like Simon. To us, Simon Vicary sounded like a nice name. But when we tested our friends, the associations ran from "Simon Legree" to "Simple Simon." As it turned out, the child was a girl and she was named Anne, by popular vote.

Hidden Conflicts Revealed

When word responses are delayed for as much as three seconds, the psychologists are intrigued; it means some hidden conflict, and the test word comes under suspicion. For example, when druggists were tested with the word "guarantee," about half of them hesitated. The reason, of course, was that the druggist usually is the final arbiter with consumers of vague guarantees made by manufacturers and the word is unpleasant to him.

Frequently, people will conceal their real reason for liking or disliking a product, say the psychologists. Mr. Leavitt describes a study he made on the attitudes of women toward sterling silver tableware:

"Our conventional interview material pointed up feelings about the durability of silver, about craftsmanship, and about tendencies to scratch easily. We weren't quite satisfied with that material so we attacked the problem with projectives. This time we picked up a different kind of information altogether. This time it was snob appeal that was important about sterling. Women wanted it for its prestige and show off value."

All sorts of refinements of projective techniques are coming into use from finger painting to play acting. Mason Haire has used the "personification method." A group of women were shown a shopping list and asked to describe the kind of housewife the listmaker was. In one list he had Nescafé instant coffee and on another he substituted Maxwell House drip ground. The gal who used regular coffee was pictured in conventional terms, but the poor housewife who bought the easy-to-make kind was reported by 48% of the women as lazy and a poor planner; 16% said she wasn't a good wife and 4% thought she was a spendthrift. This revealed the necessity for a big advertising program with specific objectives.

"Thematic Apperception"

One of the big ad agencies in the East is using "thematic apperception" by asking people to make up stories about simple pictures of people washing the dishes, cleaning a floor, or some other domestic scene. In the process the person pours out a lot of information about himself without knowing it.

To check publicity releases, Gordon Allport has used the "chain interview." A news story is read to an individual who then repeats it into a tape recorder giving his own interpretation of it. The tape recording is then played to another person and so on through a chain of six or eight. This method is said to produce very convincing findings on the way any particular company message will be received by a particular audience.

• 14 •

George[1]

LULA MAY WASH

GEORGE was in my fifth grade English class last year. He stays at our school from Monday to Friday and because his family lives in town he goes home for the week end. He is totally blind, and not to live at our school all the time is a slight disadvantage to such a child as George. It takes long and constant practice of moving in the same paths, being surrounded by the same things in their same places for a blind child to become completely oriented and feel secure and free. George has always been blind and therefore he has only a vague knowledge of the things about him, the relationships of objects and the territory in which he moves. The sensation of blindness is a feeling of vacancy beyond the realm of touch. When a blind person stands in an unfamiliar spot he feels as if he is standing on the only ground that exists and if he moves he will step out into nothingness. If he is in an unknown room filled

[1] Printed by permission.

with moving, chattering people, it is a repelling task to find an object if that requires movement in an unknown direction. Of course, these sensations are not defined by children, but some such feelings exert a pressure toward inertia.

At home George is assisted in every movement. He is placed by the radio and shown the dial. There he remains for hours listening, listening.

For the first four years of George's school life he lived in a small dormitory-style cottage that housed only twenty-five boys. He was led to his classroom across the campus by a boy with partial vision. All of his school supplies were within reach with the teacher close by if he became confused or lost.

But when he reached the fifth grade his whole world changed—he moved to the main building to live and go to school. The main building has many classrooms and long and devious corridors; each pupil is responsible for his own books, papers, seats, and stylus. In the study room there is a shelf for all the books of a certain subject.

George did not get his lessons. The history teacher said, "He's lazy." The arithmetic teacher said, "He's stupid." His word recognition was quick and accurate, but his reading was poor because he did not know the new words and he did not always obey the punctuation marks. His spelling was good on Friday because we had gone over the words in class during the week. I joined the others with this dismissal statement: "George is not stupid," I said. "He is too lazy to move."

We sent George's mother a report filled with F's and

she blamed all of us. She said we were unfair to George —we were depriving him of the privileges of the school; he should be taking organ lessons, too; George liked music, he listened to the radio all day long. Then the primary music teacher tried George again in music. In her studio he was alone with the full attention of the teacher. On the piano bench all the world of the moment he needed was within his reach. He did quite well.

I tried to put pressure on George in English class. If he didn't write his paper during the legitimate study period, he would have to take his recreation period to do it. I put him in a classroom near me and told him I would be back at a certain time. The school floor was deserted and deadly still. I went back, took the paper, and started to leave. George did not stir; before I was out of hearing he asked me to show him the way back to his quarters. Then I was almost sure I understood George's problem.

The big, strange new world of the main building and the fifth grade were too much for him to cope with. While everybody else was rushing to the bookshelf to get a book for class George was pushed aside. If he found the shelf at all, the books were all gone or if his book was a few inches out of the place he had left it, and hence it was lost to him. So he came to class without a book, and even if he had prepared his written work it also could not be found. Children are often unkind when they think they are having fun. They would move George's material to see him search in vain for it, or watch him sink back in his seat inertly. On more than one occasion I had to turn George about when he was going in the wrong direction from the classroom. His whole body would be electric with tension; he would be rigid and almost twitching.

Of all the people listed as blind only a small per cent are totally so, and those who have only object perception are immeasurably helped by it. Even so, many of those faced with George's calamity of total blindness since birth can adjust to their world better than he. George's problem has factors in it that we at school cannot change because of his home environment and long established habits of inactivity.

PART III

All speech, written or spoken, is in a dead language until it finds a willing and prepared hearer.

—Robert Louis Stevenson

• 15 •

Tennyson at Leyte Gulf[1]

FREDERICK L. GWYNN

EVEN in the air age, it is a long way from the Crimean Peninsula in the Black Sea to the waters east of Luzon in the Philippine Islands. But a strange concatenation of events occurring ninety years apart—to the day—links these places in justification of Shelley's sweeping dictum that poets are "the trumpets which sing to battle, and feel not what they inspire . . . ," and in contradiction of Auden's dogmatism that "poetry makes nothing happen. . . ." For involved in Admiral Halsey's charge south on October 25, 1944, in the Battle for Leyte Gulf is the charge of Major General Lord Cardigan's Light Brigade on October 25, 1854, in the Battle of Balaclava. And between the two actions stands Alfred Tennyson's dactylic jingle, "The Charge of the Light Brigade," as a tenuous but surprisingly effective link.

[1] *The Pacific Spectator*, Spring 1951, pp. 149–160. Reprinted by permission of author and editor.

October 25 is a day not unknown to previous junctures of sword and pen—or at least, of longbow and pen. For it is the Feast Day of SS. Crispin and Crispinian, as Shakespeare pointed out, the day on which King Henry V of England led his small band of tired and hungry archers to rout a superior French army at Agincourt in 1415. But only a happy few know Shakespeare's passage about St. Crispian's Day, compared to the multitude familiar with Tennyson's lines about another October 25 four centuries after Agincourt. Every literate Englishman and American knows that six hundred soldiers, with cannon to their left and right, charged three half-leagues onward into the Valley of Death, while all the world wondered. And while most Americans could not define a league or a light brigade, or tell you when and where the charge took place, they have the metrical phrases and the heroic atmosphere immutably fixed in the recesses of their memory.

The story of just why the Light Brigade rode into the valley, of how all the world wondered, and of the Poet Laureate's deep emotional reaction to the news of the sacrifice is still an entrancing tale.[2]

In 1854 a British Expeditionary Force, along with French and Turkish allies, was fighting the Russians on the Crimean Peninsula. By late October the English were sick and short of supplies; with a dangerous East-

[2] My account comes from the London *Times* (November 1854); Alexander Kinglake, *The Invasion of the Crimea* (1868), Vol. IV; Lieutenant General Sir George MacMunn, *The Crimea in Perspective* (1935); and C. E. Vulliamy, *Crimea: the Campaign of 1854–56* (1939).

ern winter[3] coming on, they were well aware of their failure to take the crucial fortress of Sebastopol on the west shore. Lord Raglan, the British commander, had to defend a dirty little village on the south shore—Balaclava—for it was his supply base and could not be lost to the enemy. A cavalry unit, under Lord Lucan, was Raglan's main force; it consisted of Sir James Scarlett's Heavy Brigade (heavily armed and protected horsemen) and Lord Cardigan's Light Brigade. There were also the Scottish 93rd Highlanders, under Sir Colin Campbell.

The Highlanders were the first British troops to distinguish themselves in the Battle of Balaclava. Early on the morning of October 25, some 25,000 Russian soldiers advanced on the town. "You must die where you stand," Sir Colin told his regiment, placing it in the famous "thin red line" of two men deep. Two volleys from this line's guns temporarily broke up the Russian cavalry, but the enemy soon came on again. Then, for no apparent reason, it paused. The lapse was but one of many on the part of General Ivan Liprandi, the Russian commander.

By this time General Scarlett had his 900-horse Heavy Brigade in position, and he ordered a charge—uphill—against 2,900 Russian cavalry. In just eight minutes the Heavy Brigade (led by the 300 Dragoons

[3] The severity of that winter of 1854–55 is attested even today by the existence of the "raglan" overcoat, the "cardigan" sweater, and the "Balaclava" face-helmet. Even the beards which we associate with mid-Victorian faces were grown during a fad of imitating the unshaven heroes of the Crimea.

celebrated in Tennyson's less-known poem) had repulsed the superior force.

Now, Lord Raglan could see all this taking place. He and the allied French commanders, their staffs, and the war correspondents—including the renowned jingoist W. H. "Billy" Russell of the London *Times*—were all comfortably ensconced on Sapoun Ridge, looking down on the mile-long valley. It was like a seat on the fifty-yard line: when the Highlanders and the Heavy Brigade harried the enemy, the party on Sapoun Ridge cheered them on.

But Lord Raglan saw that the Russians were far from defeated. Indeed, they still held the redoubts on the hills that formed the valley, and Raglan apparently spotted evidences of gun movement there which the English cavalry down in the valley could not see.

And so the notorious Order No. 4 went down to Lord Lucan. It was written by Colonel Richard Airey, Lord Raglan's Quartermaster General, and delivered on horse by Airey's aide-de-camp, Captain Louis Nolan. It was a monstrously vague order: "Lord Raglan wishes the cavalry to advance rapidly to the front, follow the enemy, and try to prevent the enemy carrying away the guns. Troop of horse-artillery may accompany. French cavalry is on your left. Immediate." The order failed to locate either the front, which was so plain to the general staff and spectators on Sapoun Ridge, or the guns, or—accurately—the French cavalry.

So far as we can tell from the testimony later presented to Parliament, Captain Nolan came dashing up to Lord Lucan with a great flourish of eagerness and an air of immediacy. Lucan read Order No. 4. Then he looked up the valley, at the end of which General Liprandi had placed cavalry and a dozen guns, and—seeing no Russian movement of "carrying away" cannon—asked Nolan for the location of the guns. The junior officer, who was famous in the Army for sanguineness and high spirits, foolishly lost his temper; pointing vaguely up the valley instead of at the adjacent hills, he spouted: "There, my Lord, is your enemy; there are your guns!"

Quite naturally, the cavalry leader became angry too. But since he had to accept Nolan as a direct representative of the commanding general, Lucan got the notion that there was pressure on him to attack immediately and at all cost. He rode over to Lord Cardigan, commander of the Light Brigade, and in another vague conversation passed on the orders. Cardigan pointed out to his chief that there were Russian guns on both sides of the valley and that it would be dangerous to risk an attack. Lord Lucan pointed out that Lord Raglan had ordered the cavalry to go forward. Soldiers obey; theirs not to reason why.

A little after 11:00 A.M. Lord Cardigan gave the tragic order to his Light Brigade. Placing himself in the front of the lines, he led the troop into the valley. His eye was on the Russian positions over a mile distant.

At this moment a further and dramatic misunderstanding occurred. Cardigan was surprised and annoyed to see Captain Nolan suddenly gallop across the path of the whole Brigade, screaming like a madman. He may have been joining in the charge; it is more likely that he was trying to divert the horsemen toward the guns on the hills to the right—apparently the target meant by Lord Raglan. But Nolan never lived either to warn Cardigan or to explain his actions of the day. A piece of Russian shrapnel struck and killed him as the Light Brigade's gait quickened into a gallop.

Into the jaws of death and the mouth of hell rode six hundred other horsemen. And, as Tennyson's line hyperbolizes, "All the world wonder'd." For up on the Sapoun Ridge it was plain to all that the sortie could end only in massacre. As the gallery gazed and stood aghast, General Bosquet shook his head and summed up the catastrophic Charge with Gallic gnomism: "*C'est magnifique*," he said, "*mais ce n'est pas la guerre*."

The guns of the Russian artillery and infantry on both sides of the valley threw iron at the moving body of resolute cavalry. Then the cannon at the end of the valley began firing point-blank at them. Soon the aisle was a mélange of fallen men and riderless horses. But Lord Cardigan never looked back until he had ridden (at a pace which he coolly estimated at seventeen miles an hour) into the smoke of the guns at the far reach of the valley. When he finally wheeled about, he found himself separated from the bulk of the Light Brigade, and he saw it retreating. Miraculously spared, he followed back out of the Valley of Death. The whole charge and retreat lasted about twenty minutes.

Once more the Russians mysteriously failed to take advantage of their superiority, and the remnants of the

Brigade were able to return to their own lines and muster. Of the 673 men who had charged, only 195 were still horsed. Two hundred forty-seven had been killed or wounded. Through a series of ambiguous orders, unintelligent transmission of orders, and specific tactical errors (for example, advancing a cavalry unit without support)—on the part of the commander-in-chief Raglan, the Quartermaster General Airey, the aide-de-camp Nolan, the cavalry commander Lucan, and finally the single-minded commander of the Light Brigade Cardigan—an extremely dangerous, fatal, and totally unnecessary attack had been made. Lives of men paid for errors in communication and precipitate actions. Someone—in fact, a fairly large number of responsible men—had indeed blundered.

Yet the Charge itself was glorious. Like the British longbowmen at Agincourt, the British cavalry at Balaclava met a foe far superior in numbers and tactical position. Yet there was no faltering on anyone's part. Even Lord Cardigan, an impossible man who quartered himself abroad his private yacht in the harbor while his troops suffered privation ashore, lived up to the oldest tradition of military men by immediately obeying the order as he understood it, even though it meant leading his horsemen into the cannon's mouth. Legend says that when he apologized to his depleted Brigade after the Charge, the men replied, "Never mind, my Lord! We are ready to go again!" Despite the stupidity of the Charge itself, the reply is undeniably noble. The British have made it, aloud or implicitly, a number of times before and since.

According to Tennyson's son and grandson,[4] it was a little over a month later (December 2, 1854) that the Poet Laureate sat down with a newspaper and read a report of the Battle of Balaclava. As an Englishman and as a poet he was profoundly moved. His vivid metrical sense lighted on the phrase "some one had blundered," and in a few minutes he had written the famous poem. He sent the jingling verses to the *Examiner,* a weekly magazine, where they appeared on December 9 over the signature "A. T."

Four years before, Ralph Waldo Emerson had commented on Tennyson's amazing popularity. The morning after the Laureate sends a poem to a periodical, Emerson wrote in his journal, "it is reprinted in all the newspapers, and, in the course of a week or two, it is as well known all over the world as the meeting of Hector and Andromache in Homer."[5] (Better known, we would have to say.)

"The Charge of the Light Brigade" bore out Emerson's words with a vengeance. All over the world people read, recited, memorized, and repeated the poem. Lesser poets, like Julia Ward Howe in America, imitated it. Lesser men than Cardigan's sat in homes, schools, and lyceums responding to Alfred Tennyson's stark recreation of the original nightmare. Perhaps the poem's popularity in the United States owes much to

[4] See *Alfred Lord Tennyson: a Memoir by His Son* (1897), I, 381, 386; Charles Tennyson, *Alfred Tennyson* (1949), pp. 283–284, 288–289.

[5] *Journals of Ralph Waldo Emerson,* ed. Edward Waldo Emerson and Waldo Emerson Forbes (1912), VIII, 140 (October 1850, undated).

its inclusion as a declamation piece, complete with gestures and intonations, in Epes Sargent's widely circulated *Intermediate Standard Speaker* (1857).[6] It is not too much to say that every schoolboy in the late nineteenth and early twentieth centuries has known Lord Tennyson's dramatic ode.

Ninety years after the Battle of Balaclava—to the day—a line in Tennyson's poem influenced an important decision in the largest naval engagement of all time, the Battle for Leyte Gulf. In the three days of October 23–26, 1944, the United States Navy sank twenty-eight ships of the Imperial Japanese Fleet, ending Japan's claim to being a modern sea power. Of all the myriad decisions necessary to fighting this battle, none is more dramatic than one in which the echo of a Victorian poem, written to celebrate what was after all a minor incident in a comparatively minor international altercation, crept into the brains of two men, tempering and coloring a reversal of military plans affecting thousands of American and Japanese soldiers and sailors.

The Battle for Leyte Gulf was an immensely complicated conflict. Every type of naval craft—from submarines to airplanes, from battleships to torpedo boats—took part in this struggle for the vital Philippine Islands. It was really several separate battles in one, some occurring simultaneously in widely separated areas. A brief summary of the events surrounding the incident in which Tennyson figures must oversimplify an almost

[6] See John Olin Edison, *Tennyson in America: His Reputation and Influence from 1827 to 1858* (1943), p. 103.

imponderable series of decisions, orders, and engagements.[7] But the main outlines are clear.

Soon after the American landing on Leyte Island on October 20, 1944, the Japanese Fleet threaded its way toward where the United States Navy roved in support of General Douglas MacArthur. Split into three units—the Southern, Central, and Northern Forces—the enemy was engaged by our Third and Seventh Fleets and our submarines.

The total destruction of twenty-eight Japanese ships at the expense of six American—which turned out to be a tonnage ratio of about nine to one—was possibly the biggest major naval defeat in history. And one cannot attribute this defeat to inferior Japanese strategy, sea power, or gunnery. It was the lack of coordination, the abject failure of communications, and the fact that Admiral Kurita (commander of the Central Force) retired at a time when he held the advantage that conspired to point up the superior power and courage and luck of the United States Fleet.

Yet the lapses were not all on the Japanese side. The most dramatic and ironic defection occurred at the juncture of the famous northern thrust and reversal south of Fleet Admiral (then Admiral) William F. Halsey, Jr. A mnemonic irrelevance and error in taste on the part of radio communicators misled the Admiral

[7] See James A. Field, Jr., *The Japanese at Leyte Gulf: the Sho Operation* (1947); Fleet Admiral W. F. Halsey, Jr., and Lieutenant Commander J. Bryan III, *Admiral Halsey's Story* (1947); Vann Woodward, *The Battle for Leyte Gulf* (1947); Captain Walter Karig and Others, *Battle Report: the End of an Empire* (1948).

into making what he has maintained was his only mistake in the long and complicated battle.

Halsey's Third Fleet, according to the Operations Plan which Fleet Admiral Chester A. Nimitz had given it, had two missions: (1) It was, of course, to support and protect General MacArthur's landing on the Philippine Islands. (2) But further orders in the Op Plan followed traditional Navy doctrine in stating: "In case opportunity for destruction of major portions of the enemy fleet offers or can be created, such destruction becomes the primary task."

On the night of October 24 Halsey had enough information to change his mission from No. 1 to No. 2. His pilots had hit the Japanese Central Force and reported it badly damaged, its battle efficiency impaired. Other pilots had finally spotted an expected enemy carrier force to the north. Halsey therefore took his fast carriers and battleships up off the northernmost Philippine island to meet what he considered the major Japanese threat. In so doing he left Vice-Admiral Thomas C. Kinkaid's Seventh Fleet, protected only by old battleships and small carriers, in a "temporarily tight situation" off Leyte. After Halsey went north, the Japanese Central Force—much less damaged than had been reported—made its way through San Bernardino Straits to open sea and wreaked havoc on our small carriers before foolishly turning away. To balance this beating, however, the Japanese Southern Force came through Surigao Straits to take an overwhelming defeat at the hands of, primarily, our old battleships. And Halsey's

Third Fleet, together with the amazing American submarines, sank four carriers and three other ships of the enemy's Northern Force.

The unique tactical element in this tremendous undertaking was a group of Third Fleet warships known as Task Force 34. This unit, although it completely escaped the disaster of the Light Brigade, was subject to a confusion of location reminiscent of the confusion in orders at the Battle of Balaclava. And the reason for this misunderstanding lies in a sequence of unfortunate messages exchanged, or missed, by Halsey and Kinkaid —and by Admiral Nimitz, who was some five thousand miles away at Pearl Harbor.

About 3:00 P.M. on the twenty-fourth, two hours before he discovered the enemy Northern Force, Admiral Halsey prepared a formation of new battleships (including his own flagship *New Jersey*) and other gunnery craft, and designated the unit Task Force 34. Its first mission was to engage the Japanese Central Force if it sortied from among the islands into the open.

It so happened that in describing this plan, Halsey's message stated that the force "will be" formed. It also happened that Admiral Kinkaid intercepted this message and assumed that Task Force 34 was in the immediate process of coming into existence. He did not intercept Halsey's message two hours later, which read: "IF ENEMY SORTIES, TASK FORCE 34 WILL BE FORMED WHEN DIRECTED BY ME."

About eight o'clock that night Admiral Halsey walked into Flag Plot on the *New Jersey*, placed his finger on the chart north, and said, "Here's where we're going." Within a short time he had sent out plans to his forces and informed Kinkaid, Nimitz, and even Fleet Admiral Ernest J. King in Washington that he was "PROCEEDING NORTH WITH 3 GROUPS TO ATTACK CARRIER FORCE AT DAWN." Kinkaid and Nimitz assumed that these were carrier groups and that Task Force 34 was detached and guarding San Bernardino Straits. But it was not until after 3:00 A.M. the next morning (October 25) that Halsey plucked this unit from his Third Fleet to make it a subordinate entity. By this time he was racing north to meet the Japanese carriers.

An hour later Kinkaid radioed Halsey, "IS TASK FORCE 34 GUARDING SAN BERNARDINO STRAITS?" and Halsey received the message—two and a half hours after its transmission. Soon Halsey was getting frantic reports that Kinkaid's small carriers were under attack and needed help. These half-dozen messages explained that the enemy's Central Force had returned during the night to fire on the thin-skinned little carriers, and one dispatch said that Kinkaid's old battleships were "low in ammunition" (after the night's engagement with the Southern Force). This explanation of the predicament reached Halsey almost two hours after it had left Kinkaid's radio shack. Yet Halsey had already sent one of his carrier task groups toward the desperate Seventh Fleet.

By this time, moreover, Admiral Halsey's planes had been attacking the Northern Force for over an hour, and Task Force 34 (with the Admiral in the middle of it) had been advanced to engage the enemy at gunnery range and finish off ships damaged by the aerial attack. At ten o'clock the force was only forty-two miles from the enemy and closing fast. All hands were at concert pitch for what promised to be a major action. No one was more expectant than Halsey, whose long career in both wars had never included a surface engagement.

At this moment a message from five-star Admiral Nimitz was presented to four-star Admiral Halsey. It was simple but powerful: "ALL THE WORLD WONDERS WHERE IS TASK FORCE 34?"[8] It was one of the most unusual dispatches a combat commander on the periphery of battle could receive from a superior officer. "I was stunned as if I had been struck in the face," Halsey has said. "The paper rattled in my hands. I snatched off my cap, threw it on the deck, and shouted something that I am ashamed to remember."

To the sanguine and sensitive admiral—who had been fighting the Japanese since December 7, 1941, and who was just about to close with them point-blank at a crucial stage in the biggest naval battle of all time—Nimitz' message, with its twisted Tennysonian tag, seemed a cruelly sarcastic rebuke. Its tone implied that Halsey had made a poor disposition of his forces and that he should have been broadcasting his every move for the whole world to judge. It further implied that Halsey should turn away from his quarry (now just forty miles away!) and take Task Force 34 nearly four hundred miles to support Kinkaid's fleet, a fleet over which,

[8] Dispatches must usually be paraphrased for publication. This one is reproduced verbatim by special permission of the Security Section, Office of Public Information, United States Navy.

in the inefficient system of divided command then still obtaining, Halsey had no jurisdiction. And in effect, the melodramatic message seemed to cancel the part of Nimitz' original operation order that most appealed to the fighting Halsey—the primary task of destroying the major portion of an enemy fleet. "For the first time in over three years of fighting," Halsey says, "we had the bird in our hand, and the pressure was on me to let it escape."

And so Halsey obediently turned around and headed south with Task Force 34 and one carrier group. He reached San Bernardino Straits after midnight. Three hours before, Admiral Kurita had ingloriously taken his Central Force back into the island seas to escape, although Halsey's pilots were able to do further damage to it in the morning.

And what of Task Force 34 itself, the powerful four battleships, five cruisers, and fourteen destroyers? In supreme irony, this unit "spent the 24 most critical hours of the three-day battle steaming 300 miles up the coast of Luzon and 300 miles back between two enemy forces without firing a shot at either, though narrowly missing contact with both."[9] It was not only a bitter disappointment to Admiral Halsey and his subordinates; it was an unfortunate military move. One must reiterate the fact that the Admiral has described his breaking off and returning south as "the only mistake I made in the three-day battle," although Admiral King, then commander-in-chief of the Fleet, assured him that it was not a mistake.

[9] Woodward, *The Battle for Leyte Gulf*, p. 220.

If it *was* error, it fortunately was not disastrous, and it was based on doctrinal obedience to Nimitz' orders as understood. Yet one of the most interesting paradoxes of the greatest war in history is the fact that the crucial message that turned Halsey away from the Northern Force was *not* an order from Admiral Nimitz and *not* a sarcastic rebuke. It was a responsible superior's request for information, colored by another sailor's unconscious and unfortunate poetic reminiscence.

It was not that Admiral Nimitz, like General Wolfe before Quebec, would rather have written a famous poem than take a military objective. It was simply that one of the radio communicators at Pearl Harbor—may he ever be nameless—followed the conventional cryptographic device of padding important messages with apparent nonsense ("nulls") to aggravate the possible task of enemy decoding. The Tennysonian "ALL THE WORLD WONDERS" was not part of Nimitz' request. It was airy fluff designed to disguise a hard kernel of technical communication. Yet its semantic fate was to harmonize all too well with Nimitz' question and to color Halsey's reaction on reading it. It "sounded so infernally plausible," Halsey has said, "that my decoders read it as a valid part of the message." And it sounded infernally like a scolding.

The jingling of Alfred Lord Tennyson's "Charge of the Light Brigade," which has rung in the ears and memory of the past century, had apparently trembled in the consciousness of the encoder and burst into ether-shaking expression. Almost any other familiar line of

English or American poetry would have served the purpose and not confused the issue.

Given the battles of Balaclava and Leyte Gulf for comparison, a military historian would probably concentrate on the inept tactics of leaders whom I have barely mentioned. Both General Liprandi, commander of the Russian force in 1854, and Admiral Kurita, commander of the Japanese Central Force in 1944, failed to press a military advantage when they held it, much to the relief of the British at Balaclava and the Americans at Leyte. The historical critic might go on to analyze the similar difficulties in communication—that omnipresent bugaboo of all warfare: how the course of battle would have changed had Lords Raglan and Lucan, Admirals Halsey and Kinkaid been in better touch with one another. Such a critic might compare the roles of Captain Nolan and the staff communicator who added such a powerful catalytic agent to Nimitz' harmless query.

But for the present, one has merely outlined the weird contrast between the earnest motives of the Poet Laureate of Victorian England in writing that poem, and the potent effect its mnemonic meter and phrase had on a war so far removed in time, space, and substance from the Crimean struggle. Poets may not be the legislators of the world, as Shelley asserted them to be, but they certainly can cause a lot of trouble.

• 16 •

Arno Annello, Machinist[1]

FRANKLIN E. FOLTS

THE standards department of the Schoonway Machine Company recommended that Arno Annello, who operated a battery of automatic gear-cutting machines, be discharged for failure to attain required minimum production as set by the standards department. The foreman in whose department Annello was employed objected to the recommendation. The matter was placed before the production manager for final decision.

Arno Annello came to this country from Finland. He had received the equivalent of a grade-school education in his native land but had practically no knowledge of the English language. He secured a job as a floor cleaner in the Schoonway plant. He showed himself to be industrious and thorough, and the foreman of the milling and gear-cutting department became interested in him.

[1] By permission from *Introduction to Industrial Management*, by Franklin E. Folts, pp. 449–452. Copyright 1949, Third Edition. McGraw-Hill Book Company, Inc.

One day he suggested to one of Annello's friends that the floor sweeper should apply for a better job. When Annello heard this, he signified his desire to become an operative of the automatic sharpening machines. These machines were used to sharpen the teeth of cutters after the cutters were otherwise finished. They were automatic in operation, and with proper setup there was very little danger of spoiling the work. The foreman or an experienced assistant personally supervised each setup. The operative inserted and removed the work, started and stopped the machines, and dressed the emery wheels when necessary. He operated from four to eight machines, depending on the character of the work.

When a vacancy occurred in the department, the foreman decided to give Annello a chance, and obtained his transfer (on trial) from the cleaning department. Over a period of several months, Annello, with the assistance of the foreman, became proficient in operating the machines, and he was given a permanent job. For the next two years Annello showed steady improvement. He became known in the department as a first-class operative of automatic cutter-sharpening machines and finally developed into a skilled machine setter. While he improved as a machinist, Annello showed no aptitude in mastering the English language, and any extended or involved conversation had to be handled through an interpreter. The foreman, however, believed that Annello had the makings of a first-class machinist and was willing to put up with this inconvenience.

The company decided to install a new battery of gear-cutting machines for milling the teeth in cutters, and the foreman was confronted with the task of getting additional operatives to run these machines. The work of operating the automatic gear-cutting machines required considerably more skill than was necessary to run automatic cutter-sharpening machines. The machine attendant had to set up the indexing mechanism for the cutter blank, set the tooth-milling cutter at the correct distance off the center line of the blank, see that the cutter was properly sharpened, and set the machine for the correct stroke. The machine fed and indexed automatically, but considerable care was necessary on the part of the operative to keep the indexing at exactly the proper adjustment. The foreman approached Annello with the suggestion that he prepare himself to work on the new machines. Annello was highly pleased and put in all his spare time trying to familiarize himself with the work. He succeeded so well that by the time the machines were finally installed the foreman felt that Annello was sufficiently qualified and gave him a place on the new battery. Here Annello worked along with the other workmen, all of whom had been trained at one time or another by the foreman. He appeared to do average work and was well liked by the other men.

The standards department of the Schoonway Machine Company decided to institute a series of studies relative to the operations of gear-cutting machines for milling teeth in cutters. After the routine research had been made, the standards engineers announced the minimum amount of output which a worker must attain in order to be considered efficient. No bonus could be earned until this standard was exceeded.

During the period in which the studies were made, Annello was nervous. He appeared unable to keep his machine in proper adjustment. The pieces which he turned out were inferior in quality, and the total number gradually fell below the point at which the minimum standard was finally set. Engineers from the standards department, knowing that Annello was a protégé of the foreman, sought to ascertain the cause of his trouble, but he was unable to make an intelligible explanation. They warned him of the seriousness of the situation. For several days there was no change. Then, at the suggestion of the foreman, time-study men retimed Annello, in an endeavor to find the cause of his failure. His showing was worse than ever. The engineers began to question whether or not he had the native ability to do the work. The head of the standards department expressed that doubt to the foreman. The foreman insisted that Annello was a first-class workman. The standards department believed that the foreman was prejudiced because he did not object when they suggested that Joseph Smith be discharged. Smith had been employed on the new battery for about the same length of time as Annello and his output was not so low.

With their watches concealed in their pockets so as not to arouse Annello's suspicion, the time-study men clocked him for a third time. Still he showed no improvement. After that, the standards department became insistent that Annello be discharged. The foreman was obdurate, and the standards department appealed to the production manager for a final decision. The latter listened to the recommendations of the standards department and to the objections which the foreman raised, and then made a ruling that at the end of one week the standards department was to make another clocking of Annello's work. If it still was unsatisfactory, the foreman was to be given an additional week in which he could take any measures he chose in attempting to bring the machinist's work up to standard. If he failed to do this within the allotted period, Annello was to be fired for inability to attain the minimum standard.

At the end of the first week the new timings were made. Annello showed no improvement. When the foreman received this information, he went to Annello accompanied by a friend of the latter's, who acted as interpreter. The foreman told the machinist that his work was coming along well and that he had no need to fear the time-study men, that they would bother him no more. He said he would see to it personally that nothing happened to Annello and that as long as he tried his best he always could have a job with the Schoonway Machine Company. Annello thanked the foreman profusely and said that he always tried to do his best. The next morning he appeared at work smiling and happy. His output for the day was just at the minimum standard, but the quality was excellent. The next day his output increased. At the end of the week he was earning a good bonus. Six months later the standards department, as well as the foreman, rated him as the best worker on the automatic gear-cutting machines.

• 17 •

Ewing Condemned on Towle Action[1]

Social Workers Score Federal Official for Destroying Copies of Pamphlet

LUCY FREEMAN

ATLANTIC CITY, May 17—The leading social work educators of the country sent a message today to President Truman condemning the "arbitrary" action of Oscar R. Ewing, Federal Security Administrator, in ordering the destruction of all copies of "Common Human Needs."

This is a Federal Security Administration pamphlet written at the administration's request by Charlotte Towle, internationally famous social work leader. She is professor at the School of Social Service Administra-

[1] *The New York Times*, May 18, 1951, p. 30. Reprinted by permission.

tion, University of Chicago. Copies of the message went to Mr. Ewing and the American Medical Association.

The American Association of Schools of Social Work, an associate group of the National Conference of Social Work, which is holding its annual convention here, unanimously adapted a resolution expressing "sharp displeasure" from Mr. Ewing's "arbitrary and unwarranted act."

This is the first official action taken by the social work profession, which has been concerned since the destruction last month of 3,600 copies of the pamphlet on the order of Mr. Ewing. It was a manual for social workers first circulated by the administration in 1945 before Mr. Ewing became administrator. The administration authorized a reprint in 1949 after Mr. Ewing took over.

Study Called Un-American

The American Medical Association, on receiving reprint copies, denounced the pamphlet as "viciously un-American." Dr. Elmer L. Henderson, president, charged in a telegram to Mr. Ewing that a passage in the pamphlet advocated state socialism. The passage read:

"Social security and public assistance programs are a basic essential for attainment of the socialized state envisaged in a democratic ideology, a way of life which so far has been realized only in slight measure."

Helen R. Wright, newly elected first vice president of the National Conference of Social Work, and dean of the School of Social Service Administration, Univeristy of Chicago, made public for the first time a letter she sent to Mr. Ewing. In it she said:

"I hope I do not need to tell you that Miss Towle was not advocating or endorsing a Socialist state. The total context of the report makes it clear that she was using 'socialized' in the sense of the first definition in Webster's Dictionary; namely, 'to render social, especially to fit or train for a society or social environment.'

"The sentence could quite easily be rewritten to make that meaning clear. Parenthetically, may I remark that I do not know whether the repeated misinterpretation has been wilful or caused by ignorance. The term 'socialize' is widely used in educational and social science publications with the meaning that it was here.

"If your reason for destroying the publication was to appease the group who misinterpret a phrase or even object to the philosophy expressed by the pamphlet, I think you have taken an untenable position. If you believe the pamphlet is 'un-American,' how could you have sanctioned its reprinting? If you do not believe it is 'un-American,' how can you justify your action when other courses were open to you?

"I think the issues, involved, however, transcend the importance of this one publication. If the United States Government sets an example of destroying publications because they contain one sentence which—out of its context—can be and is misinterpreted by some people, where is this going to lead?

"It is not a very long step to the censoring of textbooks and other publications, such as was the practice in Nazi Germany and is the practice of Communist Russia. At this particular time it seems of special importance to keep this truly 'the land of the free.'"

Miss Wright told reporters that the action of Mr. Ewing was regrettable not only because it involved suppression of a book but because it was a blow to the whole philosophy of social work.

Towle Work Praised

The resolution said that "for many years the written productions of the creative and imaginative labors of Charlotte Towle have served as the guide, inspiration, and stimulation of the entire field of social work."

It declared the usefulness and soundness of the pamphlet that was destroyed "are universally acclaimed by student, teacher, and practitioner in the field of social work."

"It is of no small concern to social work educators that an arbitrary step has been taken by the administrator of one of the important public social work agencies of the land—the Federal Security Agency—to stop reprinting this important book; and further, the taking of the indefensible step of ordering the destruction of all copies remaining in stock, both of which actions are presumably based upon taking one sentence out of context and yielding to unwarranted pressure from persons and groups ill equipped to pass judgment on the merits of this work."

Psychologists Lay Censorship to U.S.[2]

Ewing's Ban on Social Work Book Because of Use of Word "Socialized" Is Protested

LUCY FREEMAN

CHICAGO, Sept. 5—The American Psychological Association defended the social work profession today against "unwarranted Government censorship."

The action stemmed from an order last April by Oscar Ewing, Federal Security Administrator, that publication of a Government book written by a leading social work educator be stopped, and the existing stocks be destroyed.

The Council of Representatives of the association, the governing body, at the closing session of the organization's annual meeting, directed that a letter be sent to the American Association of Social Workers, with copies to Mr. Ewing and Charlotte Towle, author of the book, "Common Human Needs," urging the social work group to reproduce the book, which is not copyrighted. The letter also protested Mr. Ewing's action.

Psychologists Offer Aid

Miss Towle, who teaches social work at the University of Chicago, wrote the book in 1945 at the invitation of the Government. Mr. Ewing banned the book after the

[2] *The New York Times*, Sept. 6, 1951, p. 33. Reprinted by permission.

American Medical Association objected to the use of one word in it—"socialized."

Miss Towle has said that she used the word in its strict sociological sense, to mean integrated and more fully social, and not in any political concept. She offered to remove the word from future editions.

The psychological organization asked the social work association whether any assistance would be needed in reproducing the book and said that "if so, we'd like the opportunity to see what we can do."

Fillmore H. Sanford, executive secretary of the psychological association, who drafted the letter, said that the psychologists felt that "censorship of any sort, once you start it, can destroy intelligent thinking on which democracy rests."

"We feel that this book should now be available to those who want it," he added. "The appearance of one word that might possibly lead to misinterpretation is no excuse for destroying a valuable book."

• 18 •

The Conquest of Fear[1]

FREDERIC M. LOOMIS, M.D.

When I saw the name of the patient listed for 3 o'clock that afternoon, I looked forward with pleasure to the visit. She had been a sweet and pretty thing when I put her first and second babies in her arms. Now, glancing at her history, I was surprised that she had not been in for a routine checkup for nearly five years. On her last visit, she had been about 35.

When she entered my office at 3 P.M., I could hardly believe my eyes. She looked not five years older, but 15. Instead of a gay smile, there was stark fear on her face. When she found her voice, she said, "I have some bad news. I just had to talk to you about it."

"Martha!" I said. "What has happened? Your husband? Your children?"

"No," she replied, "not as bad as that—just me. Remember how active I used to be? Golf, tennis, having

[1] Excerpted from *Coronet*, July 1949, pp. 19–21. Copyright 1949 by Esquire, Inc.

babies, and doing all my own housework besides? Well, about six months ago, when we returned after living out of town for a few years, I got short of breath on that same golf course. I began having what I thought was heartburn when I went up those hills.

"After a while I noticed that the same thing happened when I hurried to the car after I had been sitting quietly in a theater or at a lecture. And the other night Junior was so naughty that I got terribly upset. Then the heartburn came on again worse than ever—and I hadn't even moved!"

"Pain in your arm, too?" I asked.

She looked up in surprise. "Why, yes! And I was so uncomfortable that my husband insisted I go to our family doctor. After I talked to him, he just listened to my heart and took my blood pressure. Said they were pretty good, but then he sent me to the hospital for an electrocardiogram. You can't guess what the specialist told me when he got the report."

"I don't have to guess—but go on," I answered.

"*Angina pectoris,*" she said in a tragic voice. "Then he said something about spasms, but I didn't half hear because I knew that angina meant a terrible death. At home, I looked in the dictionary and it said 'a painful disease characterized by a sense of suffocation in the chest.' That's me, all right!

"Next day, I went back to our family doctor and he said, 'Don't fight it. You can't lick it. On your way home, get some nitroglycerin tablets—here it is written down—and put a tablet under your tongue when you feel the pain coming.'

"I haven't slept a wink since. I keep thinking about my children without a mother. . . ."

"Did you get the nitroglycerin?"

"No," she said. "I was afraid it would explode or something. What's the use, anyway?"

I took a small brown bottle from my pocket and tossed it across the desk. "Try some of mine," I said. "I've had tablets like that in my pocket for ten years. I started exactly as you did—even thought it was heartburn. As to that word 'spasm'—it doesn't mean you are going to have fits. Your doctor said spasmodic angina. That means that the blood vessels supplying the heart itself have a spasmodic contraction after sudden exertion or too much emotion.

"Then, because the channel is suddenly smaller, the heart doesn't get enough blood for the moment and *tells you so* by pain. It's like a traffic signal—when it says STOP, it means it—but like that red light, it changes pretty soon. Nitroglycerin just helps to change it more quickly by relaxing the tension in those little arteries."

"But," she exclaimed, "you can't be serious about yourself! I can't believe that you . . . and for ten years . . . you look so well and strong . . . how about those things you see in the paper every day?—dropped dead of heart disease, died in his sleep, collapsed on the golf course? . . ."

"Martha," I said, "I've been through this whole thing. Now listen to me. I gave up bringing babies into the world because I knew that if a terrific complication arose suddenly, my heart might tighten up so badly that

I could lose the mother and child before I got help. It almost happened once—and that was enough.

"I also gave up quite a lot of other things that had seemed important, but I soon learned that practically every one of them could be replaced by something useful and pleasant that did not involve sudden strain. I could walk but I couldn't chase a streetcar, and as soon as I learned that lesson I was happy again.

"If I feel the beginning of a pain, I stop in my tracks —no matter where I am or who sees me—take one of those little tablets, and wait till the light changes."

"You mean I must carry those things with me as long as I live?"

"Suppose you do? You carry a compact, don't you? . . . However, there's something else you will have to carry that's much more important."

"What is it?" she cried.

"A little different philosophy of living, my dear. You can be a good wife and mother, and be happy too, if you stop rebelling at what you think is a 'terrible' fate."

• 19 •

Kids Believe the Darnedest Things[1]

ROBERT M. YODER

If your son or daughter, the sunshine of your days and the bane of your nights, feeds an occasional piece of buttered toast to the radio or pours a glass of refreshing fruit juice into the loud-speaker, it is not necessarily a sign the little darling is working up to be a juvenile delinquent and prepping to burn schoolhouses. On the contrary, it probably indicates a kind and friendly disposition. The chances are strong your tot believes that little men, say two inches high, reside in the radio and are responsible for all that clamor.

This is one of the most common deductions children make as they set out to comprehend this peculiar world. You will, of course, apply what disciplinary measures occur to you, but if you are cross with the child, you

[1] *The Saturday Evening Post*, Oct. 30, 1948, pp. 28, 112, 113. Reprinted by permission of the author and editor.

will depress Mrs. Ada Campbell Rose, who has become a sort of surprised authority on the strange misapprehensions children live under.

Mrs. Rose is putting in her tenth year as the editor of a magazine for children—*Jack and Jill,* the smallest member of the Curtis family of magazines and therefore the *Post's* bright-eyed kid brother. Started in 1938, *Jack and Jill* is about the same age as a great many of its readers. In those ten years Mrs. Rose has become the confidante of children all over the world. They write her some 18,000 letters a year, as contributions to the magazine.

One subject highly popular with the kids is a running category called, "I used to think." In this, from the wisdom of eight, nine, ten, or eleven years, the children tell of the misconceptions they entertained when they were just kids—erroneous beliefs that seem funny now. The belief that there are little people in the radio is one of the most common. If your tot shares his soft-boiled egg with a $500 radio-phonograph combination, you may find some consolation in knowing that he is one of thousands with the same idea, and that it is a gesture of friendliness, not pure vandalism; though vandalism, too, is mighty popular at that age.

The several thousand "I used to think" letters Mrs. Rose has received make up a body of misconstructions that are usually just as logical as they are funny. The children of many lucky parents keep quiet while the radio is playing—until they learn better—because they think the performers can hear you. They applaud because they suppose the performers can hear that. The idea that the radio is inhabited is as general as the belief that a quarter of an hour is twenty-five minutes. If you will say that to yourself three or four times, you will be unable to see anything wrong with it. It may not be true, but certainly it is more logical than having a quarter of an hour last only fifteen minutes. As for the two-inch people in the radio, are they any more fanciful than some of the six-foot people in the radio studios?

Another standard "I used to think" is that when it rains around your house, it is raining everywhere. All the visible evidence is in support of this proposition, and the error does credit to the child's intelligence. Furthermore, a universal rain would be a lot fairer shake.

It is a strange world the children live in, in their early struggles to decode adult concepts and adult words—words which are often two-faced little liars, and don't mean what they say or suggest. The letters to this department of *Jack and Jill* help explain—too late—things that may have baffled many of the correspondents' parents. Things might have been easier for one mother, for instance, if she had known a fact her daughter later wrote Mrs. Rose about. For a long time this girl thought her family was rolling in dough. Every time her mother mentioned rich food, she supposed it meant expensive food. And things would have been a lot more clear to another mother if she had known for what strong and valid reasons her son opposed spinach. He thought it was made of old tea bags. This can't be true, can it?

Mrs. Rose's young friends confess to staggering along under a remarkable load of misconstructions, all of which they now find laughable, although it is interesting to note that their most fantastic conclusions have a certain plausibility, and often are an improvement on the truth. Indeed, in a good many instances the youngsters would do well to cling to the error and let verity go jump in the lake. If the children's ideas were correct, this would be a somewhat delirious world. But possibly, as they ponder adults and adult behavior, they come to expect a good deal of nonsense. Here are some characteristic "I used to think" items—interpretations placed on words and events by various young ladies and gentlemen of the sand-pile-and-snow-suit set. They believe, for instance:

—That all milk comes from the same hard-working cow.

—That when adults speak of a veterinarian, they mean a doctor who treats carrots and vegetables. (The child of an amateur gardener, no doubt, whose father's garden could use a few treatments.)

—That the strange name for men and women, as distinguished from dogs, cats, and the Easter rabbit, is "human beans."

—That a chairman is a guy in a theater or restaurant who takes care of the chairs.

—That a bird dog must be quite a sight, with those wings.

—That there should be polka dots on a foot that is asleep.

—That policemen literally pinch people they are arresting.

—That firemen clanging by are on their way to burn down a house.

—That the holes in Swiss cheese are made by industrious Swiss mice.

—That Cedar Rabbits, Iowa, must be a mighty picturesque town.

—That holidays are days on which to go out and holler.

—That the letters S, M, T, W, T, F, S, always seen on calendars, spell a word, though one difficult to pronounce.

—That the proper name of this great nation is The Untied States.

—That it is unexpectedly nice of filling stations to provide rooms for tired people.

—That pepper is black—or dirty—salt.

—That if you write fast, you'll have more paper left.

—That saddle shoes mean riding boots of some kind.

—That a horse doctor is a talented equine trained to doctor other horses.

—That the radio actor, Red Skeleton, must be a grisly sight.

—That "juvenile" means "bad," and "delinquent" means children.

—That—note the dawn of disillusion—everything in the dime store sells for a dime.

—That red letters on a calendar foretell a sunny day, black letters a cloudy one.

—That Lincoln's Gettysburg Address is where the Emancipator lived, naturally.

—That seersucker is a kind of candy available at Sears, Roebuck and Co.

—That it must be a lot of fun for mothers to go out and play on bridges, for bridge parties.

The kids are fond of telling about their early blunders because it makes them feel big. Occasionally, however, the misunderstandings they are so proud of overcoming are funnier than they think. One little girl wrote: "I used to think that when you have a maid, it means you can't go out in the kitchen." She only thinks she was wrong, and may discover when she is a withered twenty-one that either you can't go out in the kitchen or you have to go out in the kitchen to cook the maid's lunch. . . .

• 20 •

The Human Factor in the Development of International Understanding[1]

ELEANOR ROOSEVELT

IF I had known then what difficulties lay ahead and how little I knew when I went to that first meeting I would have been even more terrified than I was, and I was quite worried. But I really did not know then what lay ahead in the way of education in human relations, and how much more than just good will was needed. I feel very often now, how much more one still should learn, and I made the suggestion before our last General Assembly Meeting, which brought down upon my head expressions which seemed to say this: "Well, she used to be a sensible person. I really wonder, has she lost her

[1] From an address delivered at Colgate University March 21, 1949, as the first of the 1949 Lectures in Human Relations. Reprinted by permission.

mind." And what I was asking was, whether perhaps it wasn't time for us in the Delegation to take with us to the General Assembly Meeting a well-trained psychiatrist to sit in and watch the behavior of all of us, in all our different meetings, and then come back and tell us what we had done that they thought we might either have done better, or perhaps shouldn't have done that way at all. And perhaps they would be able to explain to us some of the things which to us were so difficult to understand.

Now I am going to start by saying to you that, of course, the great problem today is the fact that we here in this country, and in other nations too, have learned a great deal about nature, about material things, but we have not learned a great deal about ourselves; and therefore, we are at the point where instead of man's using his knowledge and his new discoveries for the benefit of mankind, it may be quite possible that man may destroy himself purely because he really does not understand himself. So that this study of the Human Factor in International Relations is not an academic study at all; it is a study which means life or death, and any possible way in which we can increase our understanding we should take, and we should use, because this understanding is a very difficult thing. I thought it was much easier when I began because I thought with good will one could always get on with people, and little by little one could learn, but there is so much to learn in the realm of human beings, and the understanding is sometimes very, very difficult.

In order to bring this down to something very concrete, I am going to use tonight a document that I am very familiar with—having been Chairman of the Commission that worked on it—and I am going to try to explain to you the different difficulties that arise in writing an international document. I think in that way I can give you most clearly the various difficulties that hamper our understanding. Now the document I am going to use is the Universal Declaration of Human Rights. The Commission on Human Rights was appointed immediately after the Economic and Social Council met for the first time, and it was decided that there would be eighteen governments represented and that the first piece of work that the Commission was to do was to write a Bill of Human Rights. Well, to any citizen of the United States that sounds like a fairly sensible thing to do, but the first thing that confronted me was that a number of delegates came up (because I had been made chairman) and said, "What is a Bill of Human Rights?" Well, I pointed to the French Bill of Rights, to our own and to the Magna Carta. They went away, I suppose, to study. But it is quite a different thing when you start to write a bill of rights and it has to cover, or at least be acceptable to, as many nations as were concerned with this particular piece of work.

Of course in the Commission there were only eighteen nations represented, the same number as in the Economic and Social Council, and they were chosen geographically so as to represent different parts of the world. I can tell you of one little incident that showed me how slow-witted I had been. When we came to the last session of the General Assembly, the delegate from

Chile, who was one of the South Americans represented on the Commission, came over to me one day and said, "Madam, you must not be surprised because the delegate from Uruguay is presenting so many amendments; you see, this Document is really an Anglo-Saxon Document and at first it shocks us from Latin-American countries." He had been on the Human Rights Commission and I realized that he felt he had achieved a great understanding because he thought this was completely an Anglo-Saxon Document. And we, on our side, thought that this was really largely representative of the other peoples—of peoples from other countries who had been represented on the Commission.

So after two and one-half years, we had succeeded in writing the first part of this bill, the Declaration. Now the Declaration is only half the bill, it must be followed by covenants because the Declaration is only supposed to set standards, voice aspirations and be accepted as something the nations will strive for, but it has no legal binding value. The covenants to follow will have to be actually ratified by all nations that accept them, and then they will have the value of a treaty. But the Declaration when we presented it from the Human Rights Commission, we thought, well, we worked on it two and one-half years, it's been through the Economic and Social Council several times, it has been the round of all the governments for comments and then the comments have been considered, why this really is quite a creditable, carefully-considered Document. Now it is in Committee Three in the General Assembly. We won't have much argument about this. It took us four weeks to pass the first three articles and we changed three words! That will give you a little idea of some of the difficulties of a universal document. Everyone who hadn't had a chance to have his say before, was going to have it on every single word, and we were going to find new difficulties. Now one of the things to remember in a meeting like the General Assembly, where now fifty-eight nations meet together and where in every committee you have one representative delegate from every nation, is that you have a committee of fifty-eight representatives, and you have a god deal more variety of peoples and of interests than you have in the eighteen nations' Commission, for instance, or even in the Council. And one thing you find is that in Committee Three which deals with educational, humanitarian and cultural questions, there are quite a number of women, and those women often come from countries where an individual woman has come to the top and reached the point where she is recognized, but where the average lot of women is well, not exactly on an equality with the men who live in that area. Well now, that brought about one of the first changes.

You know in our U.S. Declaration we say "All men are created equal." Well, that is the way this universal declaration read when it was presented to the General Assembly last September, but it now reads "All human beings are born free and equal in dignity and rights; they are endowed with reason and conscience and should act towards one another in the spirit of brotherhood." Now why does it say "all human beings" instead of "all men"? We have always thought that "all men" in our Declaration included women; it never occurred to us that it did not. But the women in Committee Three looked sternly at the chairman and said, "We move that in this Declaration it say 'all human beings' and that every other article where it mentions men it shall say 'every one or no one' because if it says 'all men' when we go home it will *be* all men." Now that was one of the first things I had to understand. I had been going on the theory that the more we got away from feeling that men and women were in opposition, the more we felt that we were working together, and the less we made lines which made it seem that we were working specially for women, the better it was. I had forgotten that throughout the world there were a great many women who needed very special attention, and these other women weren't going to let me forget it, and we started right in to recognize it then and there. And so the final statement reads "all human beings."

Now why does it say "are born free and equal in dignity and rights"? Why not "are created"? Well, because when we said "are created" we were recognizing a Divine Creator and therefore the spark of the divine in every man. But around the table of fifty-eight representatives there sat people who did not want any reference to a Divine Creator, or who thought of their religion in a different way. So we learned a lesson—a lesson that I have learned now a number of times, namely, that what you must do in a universal document is to find words that express basically the *objective* that you have, but that do not get in the way of your accepting the document. Now how could we find words that could be generally accepted? We finally said that all human beings are "born free and equal," and I can believe that the reason we are born free in dignity and rights is because there is a Divine Creator; but those who want to believe differently can believe differently. The words don't get in their way. But that is quite something to learn, and since I have come home I have had a letter from a gentleman who says, "How could you, as United States Delegate, accept Article One as it now stands when our Declaration says 'all men are created equal'?" Now it is something to learn, you know, that when you sit around the table with fifty-eight nations you don't get the thing which is perfect for the United States or from the United States' point of view. You have to try to understand what goes on and what motivates the thoughts in the heads of fifty-eight different delegates; and sometimes you wonder what stands in the way because you have nothing in your background that makes you understand it until you actually get some of them to try to explain, and sometimes they don't know how to explain because they don't know what your trouble is. We discovered that in Article Two. I would be frank to tell you that I am not even sure now whether some of the difficulty was an honest difficulty or whether some of it was a desire for delay. But I will tell you exactly what happened anyway.

Article Two reads:

"1. Everyone is entitled to all the rights and freedoms set forth in this Declaration without distinction of any kind such as race, color, sex, language, religion, political or other opinion, national or social origin, property, birth or other status.

"2. Furthermore, no distinction shall be made on the basis of the political, jurisdictional or international status of the country or territory to which a person belongs, whether this territory be an independent trust, non-selfgoverning territory, or under any other limitation of sovereignty."

What do you suppose the trouble was in that? The third word: birth. I will tell you about it because it is very interesting. Our Russian delegate used the Russian expression and I would give anything in the world if I knew Russian. Any of you young enough to learn, learn it for heaven sakes, because I would learn it now if I could find the time. I am sure that part of our difficulty in understanding is because we do not speak the same language and I am sure that the Russian requires more words to say the same thing than does English, and I am also sure that there are more variations in a word. I am sure they put different endings to it and different inflections and thus they change the meaning—we have simultaneous translation. (You wear earphones, and you have a little thing beside you that you can turn to hear the person in his own language or to any one of the five official languages.) Well, suddenly Mr. Pavlov said, "That translation is wrong. It is not what I mean." But of course none of us could help him because, as I say, I don't know Russian and I can't translate the meaning. I could do it in some other languages but I can't do it in Russian. So he and the translator had to argue out what he meant. He knows English and French perfectly well but he says he doesn't know English and his French has curious lapses. Now his French is really very good but when you reach a certain point in an argument he will turn to you and he will say, "Madam, I do not understand." That is very trying sometimes. But in this case I said, "Perhaps Mr. Pavlov would tell us how he would translate it." He thought a minute and he said, "I think the word in French is *état* and the word in English is *estate*." That would be without distinction of any kind such as état or estate. Professor René Cassin is the French Delegate and one of the people on one of their very high courts, comparable to our Supreme Court. Professor René Cassin said, "There was a time many years ago when we had *trois états*, but that time is over and I don't think it would mean much." And I thought and I said, "I really don't think it would be very clear to us, 'no distinction because of estate.' " And so Mr. Pavlov said he would accept the word "class," and I said, "Oh please, not in a universal document. I think we are trying to get rid of classes in the world so don't let's put it in this document." Finally he said, "Use the word, 'birth.' " So we all accepted birth, and then Doctor P. C. Chang, who is a very learned gentleman, who is much more particular about the English language than most of us whose native language English is, said, "If we are going to use the word 'birth' we put it after 'race.' Race, birth, color, sex." I thought Mr. Bogomolov, who had replaced Mr. Pavlov, was going to die. Mr. Bogomolov is the U.S.S.R. Ambassador to France; he was so tense and so excited when he began to argue that it couldn't possibly be there, that I began to think "This isn't honest; this is just a desire to keep us from getting through." I was wrong. Finally, after long argument he said he would accept it after the word "property." In his mind "property and birth" went together. Those were distinctions because of similar things in his mind, and when it was accepted he accepted the article, and everything was perfectly all right and he sat back in his chair with evident relief and relaxation, and all of us wondered why he was relieved and what all the tenseness and excitement had been about. And most of us don't really know to this day. At least I don't, and I think it is one of the very best examples of how little we understand what is going on in the minds of some of our colleagues, because here was I, completely sure that this had no reality at all; that it was just being done so as to keep us from getting our work done. Now that did happen very often but in this case I don't think that was so. But there you are, there are your three words, and I have tried to show the difficulty created by language. The difficulty created by evidently a meaning which the rest of us don't understand very well. . . .

• 21 •

Rosie[1]

CATHERINE MINTEER

PERHAPS every teacher should be required to move to an entirely new situation each year. I thought about that last year while adapting myself to a new teaching assignment. I wondered how long I should look at things and people with new eyes, without preconceived ideas, without those old standardized responses.

Rosie, one of my eight grade pupils, helped me answer this question. I was watching a line of tardy pupils straggle down the hall while talking to the gym teacher. He was a kindly young man and seemed to want to tip me off about what to expect at this school. "We have a grand bunch of kids," he said, "nothing like the smart alecks you had over at Washington. You will find it much easier here." "Fine," I said, "I can stand a little peace and quiet for a change." Just then a little, red-faced girl hurried by, glaring at us as she passed.

"God, what a tramp!" said my co-worker. Another

[1] Printed by permission.

teacher who had joined us said, "Trash, just trash; what can you expect from a family like the Troris? We had her brother and he was a mess. He didn't even get a diploma."

Rosie was in my home room!

At the end of the first week I checked the list of service organizations and every girl but Rosie had some duty. When I asked the sponsor, she said that was because Rosie was not dependable.

I began to sense that all was not well with Rosie and her classmates. During roll call in the morning, there was a furtive snicker, almost a jeer, when I came to Rosie's name. I ignored the sounds and waited until a recess period to ask a girl who sat near Rosie who Rosie's best friends were. This girl said, "No one, I guess. She is kind of queer. She fights a lot."

I noticed that Rosie was not included in any of the chattering, giggling groups that formed at recess time. However, she seemed to be making an effort to join, because she usually moved for the first place near the door, waiting for the group with an eager smile. Somehow her efforts were never rewarded. Someone else invariably wanted that first place and as Rosie was a small, slight girl, she readily was ousted. Sometimes a boy hurrying by would jostle her, but no matter how big the boy was Rosie would protest loudly or use her fists. After a time the flurry of disorder that seemed to center near Rosie began to annoy me. I would call Rosie's name and give her a warning look. Her usual response was a loud "Awwww, whattaya pickin' on me for? I ain't done nothin'. It was so-and-so, why'ncha tell him?"

I was determined that somehow I would reach Rosie, so when I found that she was reading at a fifth grade level in eighth grade, I set up some attractive, individualized remedial work and asked her if she was interested. She showed quite a bit of enthusiasm and planned with me that she would do the lessons she understood at home, and that we would check them together in our spare time at school.

Rosie's plans exceeded her performance. After seeing that she had completed very few units at home, we decided that she would do them in her extra time in school. Unfortunately Rosie used her spare time and the class periods and even instruction periods to try to establish some kind of social situation with the pupils sitting near her. She was tardy about five times a week. She straggled in late each day from recess. She lost her report card, and failed to return the new one. In a class of forty-five pupils Rosie was a time consuming problem.

One afternoon after school I had detained Rosie a moment to tell her how important her reading lessons were for her high school courses, and how important it would be to her everyday living to have a command of her own language. She reacted as usual, immediately saying that she was working harder than anyone around, but that I just wasn't aware of what was going on. Just then the seventh grade teacher entered the room and seeing Rosie, said, "What are you doing now, young lady? Don't think we are going to put up with you the way we did with your brother." Turning to me she said, "He didn't even get a diploma. He was one of the worst cases we ever had." And back to Rosie, "If you dare to make one bit of trouble you will be kicked out of here so fast, you won't know what hit you. Do you understand me?" And much to my surprise Rosie politely and quietly said, "Yes, Ma'am." When she left the teacher said, "Scum, just scum. You can't do anything with that family. They are worse than she is."

I wondered at Rosie's docility and apparent acceptance of that teacher's opinion. I wondered what would happen if I talked to the child that way. I asked the teacher if she thought it wise to refer to Rosie's family in such derogatory terms when she was reprimanding her. The teacher said, "That is the only language they understand. You have to get tough with them."

I had another view of Rosie during graduation practice. The carefully drilled children proceeded down the aisle in perfect order, that is, all but Rosie. Her jaw was dropping rhythmically to the beat of "Pomp and Circumstance." She moved into her place in the first row, crossed her knees, and started a conversation with her neighbor. The principal commented on Rosie's gum chewing and talking, so I called to her, feeling sure she would quickly stop both. Instead I was treated to the familiar snarl, "Whaddaya talking' about? I ain't done nothin'." Feeling rather embarrassed at the product of my English teaching and home room guidance, and hoping to settle matters privately, I said "OUT" and gestured to the door. Rosie left, protesting all the way.

About fifteen minutes later Roger, a big, good-natured boy who had been on an errand came up to me and whispered, "Rosie is in the room crying." "Good,"

I said vindictively, "perhaps she will behave when she gets back."

"Maybe," he said doubtfully, "but I don't think you should have sent her out. Her brother Jack will hear about it and make fun of her, and her brother Sam will slap her around. He is in a gang and he wants the family to be the best in everything. He never got a diploma so he wants her to be all right in school."

I said, "You don't mean that they will really slap her, do you?"

"Sure," he said, "they beat her up for everything she does."

I quickly made an excuse to get Rosie back in line and as I looked at her tiny little frame and her still defiant air, and thought of Roger's remarks, I felt that I understood many things about her that had been bothering me.

Graduation day when the pupils brought their proud, beaming parents to the reception, Rosie was missing. I did not get to meet her mother and brothers, but perhaps there was very little that we could have said if we had met.

PART IV

A very pretty quarrel as it stands.
—Richard Brinsley Sheridan

• 22 •

History of a Picture[1]

JAMES THRALL SOBY

THE barrage grows heavier against the collection of contemporary American paintings bought recently by our State Department for exhibition in foreign countries. The reactionary press has brought up its big guns. Salvo one: the State Department's art is culturally un-American—"Load! Fire!" Salvo two: the paintings are subversive, *i.e.*, Communist—"Load! Fire!" Salvo three: they are degenerate, possibly mad, certainly a waste of the taxpayer's money—"FIRE!" More shells follow, but after the third burst it requires no ballistics expert to detect a similarity between this kind of ammunition and that used by the Nazis to blast the best artists out of Germany. And there is not much we can do about it except hope that the State Department's courageous project will not be wiped out before we reach a calmer time, when the American virtues of tol-

[1] *The Saturday Review*, April 26, 1947, pp. 30–32. Reprinted by permission of the author and the publisher.

erance, curiosity, fairness, and daring will reassert themselves and put an end to such patent nonsense.[2]

Occasionally, however, opponents of the State Department's collection attempt to pick off its pictures one by one. They do so by interpreting the paintings' iconography, seeking to prove by textual reading the worthlessness or iniquity of the art our Government is sending abroad. In this connection it may be of interest to consider the case of a famous modern American picture, not involved in the State Department purchases, which was once comparably deciphered by the press.

The picture is Peter Blume's "South of Scranton," completed in 1931 and awarded first prize in the Carnegie International Exhibition of 1934, Blume being the youngest artist ever to be so honored. The painting now belongs to the Metropolitan Museum. It became that museum's property in 1942 by winning a purchase prize in the huge "Artists for Victory" exhibition; it was recently sent to the show of American painting at the Tate Gallery, London, as one of the outstanding works by a living American artist. But back in 1934, when the Carnegie award was announced, "South of Scranton" created an amazing rumpus in the newspapers, as will appear.

The evolution of the painting was clearly and simply described by the artist in a radio broadcast, afterwards

[2] On April 4 the press announced the Secretary of State had suspended foreign tours of the collection, pending an artists' committee's decision on its quality. No further funds for purchase will be allotted. Accounts of the action varied, but all stressed the charge—"a waste of the taxpayer's money." Actually the pictures were bought at great discounts. If sold today, nearly all would bring far more than they cost.

condensed and printed in the *Carnegie Magazine* (1934). During the winter of 1930–31 Blume had driven South, by way of Scranton, Bethelehem, and the Shenandoah Valley, to Charleston, South Carolina. His car was old, and he stopped often for repairs, and gradually there accrued in his mind a series of images—the coal quarries at Scranton, the false-front houses in towns he passed, a feudal-looking traffic tower, the German cruiser *Emden* anchored in Charleston harbor, its sailors doing vigorous calisthenic exercises on deck, so that they seemed to soar through the air. He decided to combine these images in a single work of art, though their origins varied as to time and place. Of course innumerable artists had done this before him—Giotto and Masaccio, to mention only two gilt-edged securities in precedent's account. There was, however, this difference to be noted: whereas the scenes in medieval and Renaissance paintings were usually related as incidents of an accepted story or legend, Blume's were assembled solely because of their dream-like perseverance in his imagination.

Even allowing for this difference, prepared by art of the preceding twenty years, it is difficult to understand the furor evoked by "South of Scranton." To begin with, the public disliked the picture exceedingly. Of roughly 5,000 votes cast in a popularity contest at the Carnegie show, only twenty-two went to Blume's canvas, while Frederick J. Waugh's "Tropic Seas" won easily with a score of 1,920. In a local sense there may have been something symbolic in the preference thus expressed, for many of Pennsylvania's citizens obviously felt that Blume should have gone farther afield for his subject if planning to treat it in this eccentric manner. Scranton resented its identification with so "unlovely" a painting, and Abram S. Galland spoke up for the city and the state in a letter to the *New York Herald Tribune* for November 5, 1934. He therein declared that he had lived south of Scranton all his life, and summarized his views as follows: (1) the place shown in Blume's picture was not to be found in Pennsylvania, (2) investigation south of the Pennsylvania border should be made, (3) why blame Scranton? Mr. Robert Benchley tried to assuage local wrath by moving the painting's locale elsewhere, in a parody published in *The New Yorker* on November 24, 1934; his article was accompanied by a self-invented graphic image entitled "The Northeast Corner of Federber and Gallos Streets, Worcester, Mass."

The Pennsylvania newspapers were quick to connect public mistrust of Blume's canvas with larger issues, and "South of Scranton" became to an extraordinary degree the subject of political interpretation. This tendency was resisted in certain quarters, however. The *Pittsburgh Press* for October 31 called Mr. Dudley Crafts Watson to task for averring in a lecture that the picture was expressive of the New Deal. Not even the Republican Governor Pinchot, the paper declared, could fairly blame the Democrats for that "famous libel on Scranton."

But such ideological restraint was soon swept aside by a flood of political conjecture, and the same newspaper's Douglas Naylor, looking hard at the picture's flying sailors, decided: "As to the men in shorts, probably it [*sic*] depicts a psychological repression—that is the way men hope to play around when the New Deal gives them a chance to enjoy life." Mr. Naylor added: "It seems reasonable to conclude that the cannon atop the queer turret is symbolic of capitalism." Residents of other states chimed in, and a taxpayer of Amityville, Long Island, published in several newspapers an impassioned letter holding the Roosevelt Administration responsible for the picture.

To those interested in a more restricted political scene, the painting was equally provocative, especially as a basis for cartoons. The *Post-Gazette's* Mr. Cy Hungerford translated Blume's German sailors into the Pennsylvania politicos, Earle and Guffey, bounding through the air with Mr. Pinchot in hot pursuit, while voters watched the proceedings from a boat deck. The most elaborate cartoon appeared in the *Pittsburgh Press* for October 21. Its title was "South of Dixmont," in reference to the city's lunatic asylum. Through the medium of photo-montage, it portrayed such Pittsburgh landmarks as the Liberty Tubes, the Banksville garbage dump, and the South Park Pool, complete with bathing beauties and "Pitt backs going through the U.S.C. line." The chief protagonist of this scene was Mr. McNair, Mayor of Pittsburgh, who was shown embarking on a jaunt to Europe, wearing a sort of yachting cap. Apparently the citizenry did not want Mr. McNair to go to Europe at all; anyway not, emphatically not, in that hat.

The Pennsylvania clergy on the whole found "South

of Scranton" a sympathetic subject for sermons on the evils of materialism, though the Rev. Thomas J. Glynn ventured an unfavorable estimate on art-historical grounds. "The cubism in this picture," he said in the *Post-Gazette*, "is easily noticed from the pyramid of coal. . . . The cubist school of art is not popular among first-class artists. Even our big, practically built skyscrapers are now being erected along artistic lines." A more typical comment was that of Dr. C. Marshall Muir, reported in the same newspaper. "Mr. Blume," Dr. Muir told his flock, "is saying the democracy of America is like unto his picture, 'South of Scranton.' . . . If Mr. Blume has experienced nothing else in America, he has experienced the fact that chaos is king, having driven out God."

But did Blume himself intend "South of Scranton" to have the political, social, or moral meaning so insistently found in it? We have his impeccable word that he did not, though he was careful to point out in another connection that the artist may not always be conscious of the symbolic content of his works. (A stratagem of many enemies of modern art is to imply, contrarily, that artists slyly conceal from the public a meaning which, if understood, would cause anger and bring retribution.) Still, it is difficult to believe that Blume was deceived in the present case, particularly since he later completed an openly political work, "The Eternal City," in which his hatred of fascism was unmistakably expressed by a green, jack-in-the-box image of Mussolini.

And no one, I think, can study "South of Scranton"

carefully without coming to the conclusion that it is simply a panoramic travel picture; for me it is brilliantly conceived and executed. Despite its dream-like elements, it is more nearly related ideologically to the painting of Scranton that George Inness completed in 1855 for the Delaware and Lackawanna Railroad than to the political allegories of, say, the modern Mexicans. Unless we consider Blume's uneasy reaction to the German cruiser *Emden* a warning of things to come, there would seem to be no "message" in the picture whatever.

Perhaps there is a lesson of caution in this for those iconographers who see all shades of red when they look today at the paintings acquired by our State Department.

• 23 •

The Hanley Letter[1]

DAYTON D. McKEAN

MOST newspaper reporters were agreed that the off-year campaign in New York State in 1950 was listless; as one of them wrote, Thomas E. Dewey was "coasting into Albany for another term" while public attention was centered on events in Korea and on revelations in the New York City police department. The quiet of the campaign ended, however, about four o'clock on the afternoon of October 16, when Lieutenant Governor Joe R. Hanley gave out to reporters at his office in Albany what purported to be copies of a letter he had written on September 5, on the eve of the Republican state convention, explaining why he was withdrawing as a candidate for the nomination for governor to accept instead the Republican nomination for United States Senator. At six o'clock the same evening the Democratic State Committee gave out photostats of this letter and of the envelope in which Hanley had sent it

[1] Printed by permission of the author.

by messenger to W. Kingsland Macy, who was then a member of Congress from the First District of New York, Suffolk County Republican leader or boss, and former Republican state chairman. The Hanley version differed from the photostat only in that Hanley had omitted the first paragraph.

The letter, written on the stationery of the lieutenant governor and bearing the seal of the state of New York, follows:

Albany, September 5th, 1950

Dear King:

After further consultation with my oculist and another who was called in for consultation, I have been forced to the position that I dare not gamble on my future.

Today I had a conference with the Governor in which certain unalterable and unquestionably definite propositions were made to me. If I will consent to take the nomination to the United States Senate, I am definitely assured of being able to clean up my financial obligations within ninety days, so that I would be clear for the first time in twenty years of my life. I am assured of an adequate living compensation if elected, in a perfectly legal and unquestionable way. Also I have an iron-clad, unbreakable arrangement whereby I will be given a job with the State which I would like and enjoy (I have been told what it is) at sufficient compensation to make my net income more than I now have. This removes all the gamble from the picture and will enable me to face the future with confidence and the knowledge that even if I lost my eyesight I would still have a comfortable living and be able to do the duties evolving [*sic*] upon me.

After long and painful deliberation and in consultation

with my whole family, I have reached the conclusion that I cannot afford to gamble with my future, as things now are. Therefore tomorrow morning I am going to announce that, if the delegates will nominate me for the office of United States Senator, I will accept.

I am not talking with you because, to be perfectly honest and frank, I have neither the courage nor the strength to do so. I feel very deeply that I have somehow let you all down and perhaps I have. If you feel bitter, I can understand why, but I can assure you that within a short time you will receive from me every cent that I owe you, and at least you will not lose that part of the investment.

I will always think of you with nothing but admiration and love. You and Mr. Gannett have been wonderful and the only bright spot in the whole terrible picture is that I shall be able, within a reasonable time, to pay you both in full.

I am humiliated, disappointed, and heartsick, but in fairness to myself, to you to whom I am indebted, and to my family, I can do nothing else. Please try to see this in the fairest light possible.

Every [*sic*] gratefully,
(*Signed*) Joe

When Lieutenant Governor Joseph Rhodes Hanley wrote this letter he was 74 years old. He had lost the sight of one eye in 1947, and the following year it had been removed; his remaining eye, as he said, was not good. He had had a long and unusual career. Born at Davenport, Iowa, he had spent his youth in Iowa and attended the State University. He served in the Spanish-American War. The year 1900 was an eventful year for him; in that one year he received his law degree from

Iowa, was admitted to the bar, ordained in the Methodist ministry, and married. Apparently he mixed the practice of the law with preaching and lecturing on chautauqua and lyceum circuits. In World War I he was a chaplain in the 157th Infantry. In 1923 he accepted a Presbyterian pastorate in New York and the following year entered the Presbyterian ministry. He had only been in New York three years when he was elected to the legislature, rising by 1939 to be house majority leader; and, in 1943, he was elected lieutenant governor. He was admitted to the New York bar in 1931. He was active in many organizations, such as Rotary International, of which he was district governor in 1925; he was a trustee of Cornell University, a 32° Mason, and past commander-in-chief of the Spanish-American War Veterans.

When on June 17 Governor Dewey had announced that for reasons of health he would not be a candidate for re-election, Hanley had seen his chance; and backed by the Macy-Gannett (anti-Dewey) wing of the Republican Party he began a vigorous speaking campaign for a man of his age seeking the nomination. He appeared to be well out ahead of other possible candidates, but the Democrats got together a fairly strong ticket with Herbert H. Lehman for United States Senator and Congressman Walter A. Lynch for governor. This ticket was endorsed by the Liberal Party. Probably great pressure was put on Governor Dewey to save the day and to repudiate his no-third-term announcement of June 17, but no testimony of any participant or other evidence on this point has been revealed. Both Lynch and Harold Ickes alleged that the chief pressure was put on the governor by Nelson Aldrich, president of the Chase National Bank of New York. At any rate, on September 4, Dewey announced his change of mind and said he would run again because of the Korean crisis.

Joe Hanley did not note in his letter where his conference of September 5 with Governor Dewey took place, how long it lasted, or whether other persons were present. Lynch later charged that the conference was held in the Roosevelt Hotel in New York, that it lasted six hours, and that William L. Pfeiffer, the Republican state chairman, joined with Governor Dewey and others in giving Hanley "a real third-degree treatment" to induce him to leave a race in which he had a good chance to win to run in one (against Herbert Lehman) where he had almost no chance.

At the Republican convention on September 7 Hanley was nominated for senator, Dewey for governor. Writing in the *New York Times* on October 17, Warren Weaver, Jr., said that, "Ever since the convention Mr. Hanley had maintained in speech after speech that he withdrew as a candidate for governor and accepted the senatorial nomination of his own free will and without any pressure being exerted on him. He had stoutly repeated that he was honored to run for the Senate." It is impossible, of course, to reconcile these speeches with the letter, particularly with the phrase, "I am humiliated, disappointed, and heartsick."

The letter was in Macy's possession at the Republican state convention on September 7, and he showed it to various persons, had it photostated, and gave "about a dozen" copies to various persons whose names he has not revealed; but he stated categorically that he did not send any copy to the Democratic committee, and for their part they said that the copies they obtained did not come from Macy.

On four different occasions, according to Macy, Governor Dewey asked him to burn the Hanley letter before it became public; he refused, however, to do so because he said it would be destroying "evidence of a crime."[2] The same day that Democratic headquarters published the full text of the letter, Walter Lynch, the Democratic candidate for governor, also made the "crime" charge. He said, "The net result of this confession, of this nefarious crime, leaves the Republican Party without a candidate for either governor or senator. . . . Tom Dewey . . . is now convicted by his own running mate of bartering one of the highest offices in the gift of the people for his own personal gain as though it were a commodity in the market place." Both Lynch and Macy relied for their allegation that the deal revealed by the Hanley letter was a crime upon section 775 of the Penal Law of New York entitled "Corrupt Use of Position or Authority," an act originally passed in 1881 but subsequently amended.[3] The statute is long, verbose, and redundant; but perhaps the following excerpt from it shows what was prohibited:

[2] *New York Times,* April 10, 1951.

[3] 39 *McKinney's Consolidated Laws of New York* 440. The statute was upheld by the New York Court of Appeals. *People v. Willett* 213 N.Y. 368, 107 N.e. 707 (1915).

Any person who . . .

2. Being a public officer or employee of the state or a political subdivision having, or claiming to have, any authority or influence affecting the nomination, public employment, confirmation, promotion, removal, or increase or decrease of salary of any public officer or employee, or promises or threatens to use any such authority or influence, directly or indirectly to affect the vote or political action of any such public officer or employee, or . . .
3. Makes, tenders, or offers to procure, or cause any nomination or appointment for any public office or place . . . is punishable by imprisonment for not more than two years or by a fine of not more than three thousand dollars or both.

In *People v. Willett* the Court of Appeals of New York had said that "The statute should be construed to include a promise to procure, or cause by the same influence or otherwise, a nomination to public office by a political convention." This would seem to bring the deal related in the Hanley letter clearly under the section 775, but no effort was made by any district attorney then or later to obtain the indictment of any of the persons involved. District Attorney Frank S. Hogan of New York (Manhattan) County declined to do anything because, he said, the letter did not originate in his jurisdiction; but if Walter Lynch was to be believed, the deal itself did take place in his jurisdiction. Lynch charged that Dewey was revealed as offering Hanley "a bribe from private funds and a bribe from public funds," and he said that even if Governor Dewey should be re-elected he would have to be impeached.

For a day after the publication of the letter both

Governor Dewey and Lieutenant Governor Hanley were unavailable to reporters. When Hanley emerged from hiding he addressed a veterans' luncheon given to Dewey and talked not about his letter but about what the Dewey administration had done for veterans. He said that he would discuss the letter on the radio, as he did. In the radio speech he said, "I, of my own volition, asked him [Dewey] to run again." This statement appears to be absolutely irreconcilable with either the words or tone of the letter. Hanley added that he had never discussed his financial affairs with Dewey (a statement which is also irreconcilable with the letter) and that the money he had referred to as expecting was to come from an insurance policy he expected to cash, plus a state pension. The reference to the job offer meant, he said, the governor's assurance that his services were of great value to the State of New York and that work would be found for him if he lost the election.

Most of the newspapers tended to pooh-pooh the letter. Only the *Times* published a facsimile of it. As Harold Ickes wrote in *The New Republic*, "Excepting only the New York *Post* and *Compass*, every newspaper published in greater New York attempted to gloss over what they would have stridently denounced as an offensive crime if committed by Dewey's opponent."[4] The *Times* editorially admitted its regret at the letter but concluded that it would continue to support Dewey; the *Tribune* said that "High issues were at stake. . . . The letter itself, undignified and unfortu-

[4] Vol. 123, December 4, 1950, p. 17.

nate though it was, remains an incident in a race run for large ends. . . ." The New York *World-Telegram* counterattacked, charging that Macy had used the letter to attempt to get the Republican senatorial nomination for himself. For this allegation Macy promptly sued the newspaper for $250,000, a suit which is still pending [1952].

The Republican organization did not, but perhaps could not, contrive a consistent or effective publicity policy toward the deal and the letter. Governor Dewey and others said that the episode was a Democratic smear, although they did not allege that the letter was written by a Democrat, and they never denied that it was genuine. On October 18 Governor Dewey, according to the *Herald-Tribune*, said, "When they [the Democrats] can make a crime stick on a Republican, hell will move over and heaven take its place." This statement, though a non-sequitur, was followed by another—that two years before Herbert Lehmann had written a sympathetic letter to Alger Hiss. Without permitting themselves to be quoted by name, some Republican leaders attempted to obtain public sympathy for Hanley by saying that several years before when his father had died he had left to Hanley $75,000 in bank stock in a bank in Muscatine, Iowa, which failed for double liability, or $150,000. This debt Hanley had met by borrowing $150,000 on a note from an old friend, C. C. Hagerman of Muscatine. It was intimated that this was the debt referred to in the letter from which Hanley hoped to be free for the first time in twenty years. On October 24, close to the election, Senator

Guy Gillette of Iowa announced that a Senate subcommittee on elections would investigate. The alleged debt to Hagerman was, as the letter indicated, not the only financial obligation of Hanley's; he also owed money to Macy and to Frank E. Gannett, owner of a chain of newspapers. In Rochester Mr. Gannett on October 17 acknowledged that Hanley owed him "some money for pre-convention" expenses, but he did not give the amount of the indebtedness. Senator Gillette said later that Hanley had owed $28,500 to Gannett and Macy as far back as August, 1949.

It is impossible to ascertain after the fact whether the Hanley letter made any difference in the Dewey-Hanley election. Governor Dewey received 2,811,683 votes; Lynch 2,246,839; McManus (ALP) 209,294. Lehman, however, won by 2,624,819 to 2,363,790 for Hanley and 191,094 for DuBois (ALP). Hanley had a big (450,451) plurality over Lehman up state in spite of the letter, but Lehman more than overcame this in New York City. Whether Lehman's state plurality would have been smaller had the letter never been written, it is impossible to say; the "seasoned observers," to use the newspaper phrase, had him the victor before the letter was published.

While the letter did not defeat Governor Dewey, it did defeat W. Kingsland Macy. In a congressional district which he had previously carried by more than 50,000 votes he was defeated by an unknown Democrat named Ernest Greenwood, a retired preparatory school teacher. Since Dewey carried Suffolk County by 39,000, and since the Democratic vote for offices other than congressman did not increase, it seems reasonable to conclude that thousands of Republicans, in order to vote against Macy, voted for Greenwood. This defeat was followed nearly a year later by Macy's loss of control of the Republican county committee in the Republican primary of August 14, 1951, and his resignation as county chairman. After this defeat he issued a statement in which he said that "the full force of the state government under Governor Dewey and his chief lieutenant, J. Russell Sprague from the adjoining county of Nassau, was leveled against us. The most reprehensible methods were employed against our local officials and through them upon the [Republican] voters in their immediate circle."[5] He did not mention what the methods were which he regarded as most reprehensible.

Even before election day Hanley was in the hospital, worn out. But he received investigators from the Senate subcommittee and showed them the note for $150,000, which had written across its face "Paid," and the initials "C. I. G."

Immediately after his successful campaign for a third term Governor Dewey took a three weeks' vacation in Florida. When, upon his return, he held a press conference, he was asked about Hanley. "My promise still holds," he said, implying that the deal mentioned in the letter was not, after all, a smear but a real agreement. He would not, however, comment further. A few days later, Leo V. Lanning, director of the New York state Division of Veterans' Affairs, announced that "at the suggestion of Governor Dewey" Hanley was to be

[5] *New York Times*, August 19, 1951.

made special counsel of the division, adding that he "will bring to the Division of Veterans' Affairs fifty years of experience in veterans' problems."[6]

On January 11, 1951, Hanley announced that he was opening law offices in Albany, and "that he would accept retainers to represent clients before the legislature."[7] Reporters asked him about the nature of his debts but got no satisfactory answer; he only repeated that they were honorable.

In mid-March it was revealed in Albany that Hanley was to receive $22,000 a year from the state in salary, expense allowance, and pension; that his son James was named to a $7,000 job in the state commerce department; and that his daughter, Mrs. Clarence Wilcox, was at an unnamed salary to serve as her father's private secretary. Kingsland Macy then observed that "every contract in the letter has been carried out."

It is perhaps an anticlimax to observe that, out in Muscatine, Iowa, Senate investigators interviewed Mr. C. C. Hagerman whose alleged $150,000 note for Hanley they had seen in Albany. Hagerman, however, declared that, while he had known Hanley years earlier, he had never advanced any money to him as a loan or a gift, that Hanley had never made any payment of any kind to him, and that the initials and the handwriting were not his. The investigators, moreover, were unable to find any record in the Iowa State Banking Department or in the Office of the Controller of the Currency of any bank stock ever owned by Joe R. Hanley or by

[6] *Ibid.*, Dec. 17, 1950.
[7] *Ibid.*, Jan. 12, 1951.

his father, John R., who had left, when he died in 1933, a net estate of $20,570. The investigators, furthermore, were unable to find that any bank in Muscatine, Iowa, had gone into receivership since 1920. When he was asked in Albany about these findings Hanley said, "I will not discuss that at all," and Governor Dewey's secretary announced for him, "The Governor or his office never had any personal knowledge of Mr. Hanley's private affairs," another statement that cannot be reconciled with the letter.

Perhaps in part because Hanley had lost, perhaps in part because of the elusive nature of the evidence and the evasiveness of the principals, the Senate subcommittee quietly dropped the whole matter. No attempt was made in New York to invoke section 775 of the Penal Law, and how much money Hanley really owed, to whom, for what reasons, and for how long may never be revealed.

• 24 •

Two Letters[1]

ARNOLD SCHOENBERG and THOMAS MANN

SIR: In his novel "Doctor Faustus" [*SRL* Oct. 30] Thomas Mann has taken advantage of my literary property. He has produced a fictitious composer as the hero of his book; and in order to lend him qualities a hero needs to arouse people's interest, he made him the creator of what one erroneously calls my "system of twelve tones," which I call "method of composing with twelve tones."

He did this without my permission and even without my knowledge. In other words, he borrowed it in the absence of the proprietor. The supposition of one reviewer, that he obtained information about his technique from Bruno Walter and Stravinsky, is probably wrong; because Walter does not know anything of composition with twelve tones, and Stravinsky does not take any interest in it.

[1] "Letters to the Editor," *The Saturday Review*, Jan. 1, 1949, pp. 22–23. Reprinted by permission.

The informer was Mr. Wiesengrund-Adorno, a former pupil of my late friend Alban Berg. Mr. Adorno is very well acquainted with all the extrinsic details of this technique and thus was capable of giving Mr. Mann quite an accurate account of what a layman—the author—needs to tell another layman—the reader—to make him believe that he understands what it is about. But still, this was my property and nobody else's.

I learned about this abuse by chance: I received a magazine, containing a review of *Doctor Faustus*, wherein the twelve-notes composition was mentioned. Thereafter, Mrs. Alma Mahler-Werfel told me that she had read the book and was very upset about his using my "theory," without naming me as author, while he includes many living persons—Walter, Klemperer, etc., not as fictitious, but as real people. I have still not read the book itself, though in the meantime Mann had sent me a German copy, with a handwritten dedication, "To A. Schoenberg, dem Eigentlichen [the real one]." As one need not tell me that I am an "Eigentlicher," a real one, it was clear that he wanted to tell me that his Leverkuehn is an impersonation of myself.

Leverkuehn is depicted, from beginning to end, as a lunatic. I am now seventy-four and I am not yet insane, and I have never acquired the disease from which this insanity stems. I consider this an insult, and I might have to draw consequences.

When Mrs. Mahler-Werfel discovered this misuse of my property, she told Mann that this was my theory, whereupon he said: "Oh, does one notice that? Then perhaps Mr. Schoenberg will be angry!" This proves that he was conscious of his guilt, and knew it was a violation of an author's right.

It was very difficult for Mrs. Mahler-Werfel to convince him that he must do something to correct this wrong.

Finally I sent him a letter and showed him the possible consequences of ascribing my creation to another person which, in spite of being fictitious, is represented like a living man, whose biography is told by his friend Serenus Zeitblom.

One knows the superficiality and monomania of some historians who ignore facts if they do not fit in their hypotheses. Thus I quoted from an encyclopedia of the year 2060, a little article in which my theory was attributed to Thomas Mann, because of his Leverkuehn.

Much pressure by Mrs. Mahler-Werfel had still to be exerted to make Mann promise that every forthcoming copy of *Doctor Faustus* will carry a note giving me credit for the twelve-notes composition. I was satisfied by this promise, because I wanted to be noble to a man who was awarded the Nobel Prize.

But Mr. Mann was not as generous as I, who had given him good chance to free himself from the ugly aspect of a pirate. He gave an explanation: a few lines which he hid at the end of the book on a place on a page where no one ever would see it. Besides, he added a new crime to his first, in the attempt to belittle me: He calls me "*a* [a!] *contemporary* composer and theoretician." Of course, in two or three decades, one will know which of the two was the other's contemporary.

Arnold Schoenberg

Los Angeles, Calif.

Sir: . . . Arnold Schoenberg's letter both astonished and grieved me. Our personal correspondence on this matter had been of a thoroughly friendly character in all its phases. Not so long ago, when I sent him the English edition of *Doctor Faustus* with my appended statement, the maestro thanked me cordially with an air of complete satisfaction, so that I was led to believe that the "Leverkuehn Case" was settled and disposed of. Now I regret to learn that it not only continues to annoy him but actually irritates him increasingly, although he still has not read the book.

If his acquaintance with the book were not based exclusively on the gossip of meddling scandal mongers, he would know that my efforts to give the central figure of the novel "qualities a hero needs to arouse people's interest" were neither limited to the transfer of Schoenberg's "method of composing with twelve tones," nor was this characteristic the most important one. Quaintly enough, he calls this technique his "literary property," though actually it should be called a musical system that has long since become a part of our cultural pattern, used by countless composers throughout the world, all of whom have tacitly purloined it from its originator. The universal dissemination and the wide employment of this technique are the very factors underlying the basic error of which I accuse myself. I sincerely believed that every child in our cultural area must at one time or another have heard about the twelve-tone system and its initiator, and that no one on earth, having read my novel, could possibly imagine that I was its inventor or was trying to pose as such. This opinion of mine, I must say, was confirmed by many Swiss, German, Swedish, and, more recently, French reviews of the book, in which Schoenberg's name was quite casually mentioned. It was he himself who enlightened me with respect to my error. Serious misunderstandings, he informed me, would result from my book, unless I did something about it. Everybody except him, he said, kept receiving credit for his creation, and, if he knew anything about the breed of musicologists, they would attribute his theory to me a hundred years from now because I had developed it in my novel. His contemporaries, he added, were withholding so much from him that he had, at least, to guard his name and fame for posterity.

His concluding word moved me, no matter how absurd his apprehension seemed. It is quite untrue that it required "much pressure" to induce me to give him due credit. As soon as I understood his concern I gave instructions to include in all translations, as well as in the German original, the appended statement which now appears in the English edition of *Doctor Faustus*. It was intended as a bit of instruction to the uninformed, and I worded it as objectively as possible. "Take note," it says in effect, "there is a composer and music philosopher living among us, whose name is Arnold Schoenberg; he, and not the hero of my novel, is the one who, in reality, thought out the twelve-tone composition method." The statement does not raise the question who is whose contemporary. If Schoenberg wishes, we shall, all of us, consider it our greatest and proudest claim to be his contemporaries.

As soon as I had received the first copies of the German edition I sent him one with the inscription: "Dem Eigentlichen ["To the real one"]. It meant: "Not Leverkuehn is the hero of this musical era; you are its hero." It was a bow, a compliment. I have always addressed Arnold Schoenberg, the uncompromising and bold artist, with the utmost respect, in personal contact as well as in my letters, and I shall continue to do so.

The idea that Adrian Leverkuehn is Schoenberg, that the figure is a portrait of him, is so utterly absurd that I scarcely know what to say about it. There is no point of contact, not a shade of similarity, between the origin, the traditions, the character, and the fate of my musician, on the one hand, and the existence of Schoenberg, on the other. *Doctor Faustus* has been called a Nietzsche-novel and, indeed, the book, which for good reasons avoids mention of Nietzsche's name, contains many references to his intellectual tragedy, even direct quotations from the history of his illness. It has also been said that I had bisected myself in the novel, and that the narrator and the hero each embraced a part of me. That, also, contains an element of truth—although I, too, do not suffer from paralysis. But it has not occurred to anyone to speak of a Schoenberg-novel.

Instead of accepting my book with a satisfied smile as a piece of contemporary literature that testifies to his tremendous influence upon the musical culture of the era, Schoenberg regards it as an act of rape and insult. It is a sad spectacle to see a man of great worth, whose all-too-understandable hypersensitivity grows out of a life suspended between glorification and neglect, almost wilfully yield to delusions of persecution and of being robbed, and involve himself in rancorous bickering. It is my sincere hope and wish that he may rise above bitterness and suspicion and that he may find peace in the assurance of his greatness and glory!

Thomas Mann

Pacific Palisades, Calif.

• 25 •

Correspondence with Mrs. Hale[1]

W. SOMERSET MAUGHAM

EVERY writer who has attained a certain notoriety receives a great many letters from persons who wish to become authors and want to know how to do it. I am going to read to you now one such letter that I received a long time ago and the correspondence which ensued. The writer was a lady who lived in Boston, which as you know, its inhabitants look upon as the centre of American culture, and in Beacon Street, to live in which is an indication of wealth and consequently of social distinction.

My dear Mr. Maugham,

I trust that you will pardon a total stranger writing to you and will give a few minutes of your valuable time to answering a question which I am going to put to you. I am

[1] From *The Writer's Point of View,* pp. 15–19, London. Published for the National Book League by the Cambridge University Press, 1951. Reprinted by permission of the author and publisher.

sure you are very busy and I would not take the liberty of asking your advice if I were not fully determined to take it. To cut a long story short my son is about to leave Harvard and has determined to adopt the profession of literature. His intention is to write chiefly fiction and I should be very grateful if you would tell me in a few words how he can best fit himself for such a career. I am anxious to do everything in my power to assist him.

Cordially yours,
Frances Van Buren Hale

I was at the time staying in New York and I answered the letter promptly.

My Dear Mrs. Hale,
Give your son a thousand dollars a year for five years and tell him to go to the devil.

Yours very faithfully,
W. S. Maugham

A thousand dollars then was of course worth a great deal more than it is now.

The lady replied by return of post.

My dear Mr. Maugham,
I am entirely at a loss to understand your answer to my letter. I do not think my request was unreasonable and I cannot think that it deserved a reply which if I hesitate to call uncivil you will not be surprised if I consider strangely flippant in an author of your standing in the literary world. I regret that I troubled you and beg to remain,

Yours truly,
Frances Van Buren Hale

To this I returned the soft answer that turneth away wrath.

My dear Mrs. Hale,

I am much grieved that you were displeased with my letter. I had no wish to be impolite and I was very much in earnest; I was brief, which I thought you wished me to be, and I gave you advice which I knew to be direct and which I thought was sensible. Your son is about to leave Harvard and therefore may be presumed to possess at least the rudiments of a liberal education. I can imagine no better grounding for anyone who desires to be a writer, and from the address from which you write I judge that he has been brought up in affluent circumstances. He will doubtless have spent most of his life among ladies and gentlemen. This is a class which from a literary standpoint rests now under a cloud, but it ventures still to exist and it is well for the writer to know its manners and customs. Your son, I suppose, has led a sheltered life and at his age can hardly have gained much knowledge of the world. I do not know how better you can help him to acquire this than by taking the advice I gave you. On a thousand dollars a year he cannot starve, but if he is of an adventurous disposition (and unless he is he will not desire to be a writer) he will often find himself penniless and so obliged to do whatever he can to earn his dinner. That is not bad training. On this sum, moreover, he can travel all over the world, but only in conditions that will throw him in contact with all kinds and conditions of men. He will not be able to afford the luxury of respectability.

Besides, in telling him to go to the devil you will have explained to him that you mean him to attach the widest possible meaning to that hackneyed phrase. If he has any spirits he will soon find an infinite number of ways and means to carry out your suggestion and in five years he will have gathered experience and an acquaintance with men and women which cannot fail to be of great value to him as a writer. If at the end of this period he cannot write then you must console yourself with the reflection that he lacks what no thought of yours nor advice of mine can give him: Talent.

Yours very faithfully,
W. S. Maugham

I did not receive an answer to this for nearly a week.

Dear Mr. Maugham,

I am sorry if I sounded a little abrupt, but I will frankly confess that I could make neither head nor tail of your first letter. Of course I see now that you had no wish to be discourteous or flippant. But all the same I don't think I quite agree with the things you say. Surely it is not necessary for an author to live in a disreputable way any more than it is necessary for a violinist or a poet to wear long hair. Miss Austen wrote her admirable novels without leaving the respectable circle in which she was born, and Mr. Henry James, whose novels I am sure you appreciate as highly as I do, never to my knowledge moved in any world but that to which he was entitled by his birth and position. It was my privilege to know Mrs. Wharton for many years and though she lived so long in France I can vouch for personal knowledge for the fact that she never ceased to be a refined and accomplished gentlewoman. I cannot help thinking this proves that there is no reason why an author should not write successful books without taking such a hazardous course as you propose for my son.

But I daresay I did not put my original question quite clearly. What I really wanted your advice about was more the technique of novel writing if you understand what I mean. That is a matter on which a young author naturally stands in need of guidance and I can only say on my behalf as well as on my son's that I should be sincerely grateful for any hints you can give him.

Yours most cordially,
Frances Van Buren Hale

I replied to this letter as best I could, and at considerable length, but I will not read to you what I wrote, since I am going to tell you later of what I said then. I received an answer after some days.

Dear Mr. Maugham,

It is very good of you to have written me such a long and careful letter, but since I wrote to you last my son, after mature consideration, has decided to go into the bond business, which with his heritage and connections is of course very much more suitable.

I do not suppose you will leave this country without coming to Boston, and when you do Mr. Hale and I will have much pleasure in making your acquaintance. I shall be At Home on the first and third Wednesdays of the month until Lent.

Yours most cordially,
Frances Van Buren Hale

• 26 •

Interview with Miss Winkler[1]

SCHUYLER DEAN HOSLETT

THIS conversation takes place in the office of Mr. Zurch, Director of Personnel for an organization employing about 3,500 persons. Miss Winkler has been reported by her supervisors as doing unsatisfactory work; they ask that she be transferred on the basis of a list of charges outlined in a memorandum. Mr. Zurch has sent for Miss Winkler, who enters his office while he is talking to an assistant about another matter. Also present in the office at the time of the interview, but presumably not able to hear the conversation and doing other work, were Mr. Zurch's secretary, his assistant, and the recorder of the interview. Inasmuch as Miss Winkler spoke in a low tone, all of her comments were not audible to the recorder, especially as she became more emotional and finally tearful but the conversation was substantially as follows:

[1] Reprinted from "Listening to the Troubled or Dissatisfied Employee." *Personnel*, July 1945, pp. 54–56, by permission of the American Management Association.

W: Did you send for me, Mr. Zurch?

Z: Yes, I did; I'll be with you in just a minute. (*Mr. Zurch continues to talk to his assistant for seven minutes. During this time there is considerable confusion in the office, with the telephone ringing often, and with Mr. Zurch becoming more and more concerned over some matter about which he talks loudly, interspersing his rather definite comments with considerable swearing. This, it may be noted, is his usual manner under stress. Mr. Zurch continues.*) Now, look, Miss Winkler (*takes several minutes to look over her file and to talk to his assistant about another matter*), you remember we talked together in March and at that time B Division was not satisfied, and since you have been with Mr. Newton, and he was not altogether satisfied.

W: He didn't tell me anything like that. (*Speaks in a low, courteous voice.*) He told me after I left that he wanted me back . . .

Z: Now you have been in C Division and there is a report on your work there. Now Miss Winkler, we take each employee and try to fit her in where she can do the best job. We realize that people sometimes can't get along because of the supervisor, or fellow employees, and we try to make adjustments. (*This comment is given in Mr. Zurch's usual direct and rather belligerent manner.*) Now you have been in a number of positions. How many have you occupied?

W: (*After thinking a moment*) Four or five.

Z: Do you agree with the comments made in this report? (*Quotes from report before him on the desk.*) "Shows little interest in work and says she doesn't care for filing."

W: (*Miss Winkler's voice is growing husky now and her response is almost inaudible, but she explains that she doesn't like filing, and that she wasn't hired to do that kind of work. She was to be a stenographer.*)

Z: We don't have the work always to everyone's satisfaction.

W: But I wasn't told that was what the job would be.

Z: But we can't give everyone a job he wants . . . (*Interview has turned into something of an argument at this point; Mr. Zurch presents next charge.*) "Deliberately slows down on the job."

W: No, I do not. (*Miss Winkler seems quite incensed at this charge.*)

Z: "Uses business hours to write letters."

W: I did that *once*.

Z: "Doesn't keep up to date with her work."

W: They put in a new system up there and the supervisor asked me to help with it and I said I would. But I couldn't keep up to date on my own work and do that too. The supervisor asked me to do this at the same time that I had more than enough work of my own to do. (*Though deeply disturbed at these charges, Miss Winkler's responses are direct; by this time, however, she is on the verge of tears.*)

Z: "Leaves fifteen minutes before 12 and returns twenty to twenty-five minutes late."

W: If I went before 12, I returned earlier.

Z: "Uses rest-room facilities on 2nd floor instead of 3rd as required by the rules."

W: They were dirty on the 3rd floor.

Z: We can't be in those rooms every minute of the day. When I went in there (*apparently at an earlier complaint*) it wasn't dirty—only a few papers thrown around. It wasn't like any bathroom at home, but it wasn't dirty.

W: I have seen it at times when you couldn't use it.

Z: Why didn't you report it?

W: I did—But that's a petty thing (*i.e., the complaint*).

Z: Yes, but it means five to ten minutes more away from your desk. Listen, Miss Winkler, I think the supervisor doesn't have an axe to grind; maybe all of these things aren't true, but a certain amount is.

W: I did the work I was told to do, but some had to be left over. They expected me to get the mail out, and certain work had to be left.

Z: That's right, but there are those times when you were away from your work. (*Mr. Zurch explains the limitations on the number of persons the organization may hire; that each girl must do her work, or the organization will get behind.*)

W: I still think the charges aren't fair.

Z: Well, tell me, are there any differences between you and Jones (*her immediate supervisor*)?

W: I'd rather not say.

Z: Don't you get along?

W: Oh, sometimes.

Z: Please tell me the story. . . . (*When apparent there will be no response*) Did you go over this with Miss Counce (*the counselor*)?

W: (*Miss Winkler replies that she did, but by this time she is crying softly, and the exact words were not heard.*)

Z: We have a reputation of being fair. We try to analyze every factor in a report of this kind. . . . You have been here two years, long enough to know the whole story. . . . Do you think you aren't in the right job?

W: I want to leave the job.

Z: (*In a milder tone*) Now that's not the right attitude. We won't get anywhere that way. Has Mr. Achen (*a higher supervisor*) ever talked to you?

W: Not once.

Z: Has the Principal Clerk of the department talked to you about it?

W: Yes, once. (*Two sentences not heard.*)

Z: Do you think your work too heavy?

W: I can keep it cleaned up at times, but not all the time. There are days when with dictation, etc., I can't.

Z: Well, why don't we have the job analyzed on a week's basis and see if there is too much for one person.

W: A week wouldn't be right; once I was behind for three weeks.

Z: Honestly, haven't you taken extra time off?

W: No, absolutely not. I've noticed other girls going out when they weren't supposed to, though.

Z: Are you getting along with other employees?

W: Yes.

Z: Well, I'll tell you, you go back upstairs after you get set. (*i.e., after she has made repairs on her face because of the crying*) Do you have any other comment to make?

W: I feel he (*supervisor*) has been very unfair about my slowing down on my work.

Z: All right, O.K., now you stay down until, let's see, it's 3:30 now, until 3:45. I'll call them to expect you at 3:45.

Mr. Zurch's comment after the interview: "This girl comes from a good family and environment and apparently feels that she has a better head than the other workers. Our problem is to get her adjusted. I disagree with this report that she purposely slowed down on the job. The fact that she didn't like filing is nothing against her; we have that trouble all the time. But there is no question that she takes time off. I think 50–60 per cent of the charges are correct and the rest is put on for a good story. We'll find that the supervisor hasn't talked to her correctly. She would be a better employee under a girl who could handle her or a smart-looking man. You noted that she was especially indignant at charges of slowing down, but not so indignant on spending extra time out.

Mr. Zurch calls the immediate supervisor and the next higher supervisor into his office to discuss the situation.

Z: What is it all about, this Winkler case?

MR. ACHEN: Her attitude is wrong. She wants to be a stenographer and she was hired as a clerk-typist and there isn't a 100 per cent steno job up there. We give her some dictation, but can't give her full time. She doesn't want to do filing.

JONES: She gets behind. (*Telephone call interrupts.*)

MR. ACHEN: She said to someone, "I'll let this filing pile up and just see what happens." I think for the good of the department she should be transferred. (*Another telephone call interrupts.*)

Z: But we can't transfer her all the time.

MR. ACHEN: We spoke to her about the restrooms, but she disregards the rules. We have given her a fair chance.

Z: O.K., thanks a lot. (*Apparently the decision is to transfer Miss Winkler to another department. Mr. Zurch goes off to a meeting.*)

• 27 •

Soviet Suspicions[1]

WINSTON S. CHURCHILL

WHILE all the vexations of the Soviet abandonment of the spirit of Yalta were the subject of the prolonged correspondence set forth in the preceding chapter, a far more bitter and important interchange was taking place between the British and American Governments and the Soviets. It has been advisable to recount these issues in separate chapters but it must not be forgotten that the events recorded reacted continually and forcibly upon each other.

By the middle of February [1945] the Nazis realized that defeat was near. The advance of the Soviet armies, Alexander's victories in Italy, the failure of their counter-attack in the Ardennes, and Eisenhower's march to the Rhine convinced all but Hitler and his closest followers that surrender was imminent and un-

[1] From *Triumph and Tragedy*, Book Two, ch. 7, Boston, Houghton Mifflin Company, 1953. Reprinted by permission of the copyright owner.

avoidable. The question was, surrender to whom? Germany could no longer make war on two fronts. Peace with the Soviets was evidently impossible. The rulers of Germany were too familiar with totalitarian oppression to invite its importation from the East. There remained the Allies in the West. Might it not be possible, they argued, to make a bargain with Great Britain and the United States? If a truce could be made in the West they could concentrate their troops against the Soviet advance. Hitler alone was obstinate. The Third Reich was finished and he would die with it. But several of his followers tried to make secret approaches to the English-speaking Allies. All these proposals were of course rejected. Our terms were unconditional surrender on all fronts. At the same time our commanders in the field were always fully authorised to accept purely military capitulations of the enemy forces which opposed them, and an attempt to arrange this while we were fighting on the Rhine led to a harsh exchange between the Russians and the President, whom I supported.

In February General Karl Wolff, the commander of the S.S. in Italy, had got into touch through Italian intermediaries with the American Intelligence Service in Switzerland. It was decided to examine the credentials of the persons involved, and the link was given the code-name "Crossword." On March 8 General Wolff himself appeared at Zürich, and met Mr. Allan Dulles, the head of the American organization. Wolff was bluntly told that there was no question of negotiations, and that if the matter were pursued it could only be on the basis of unconditional surrender. This information was immediately conveyed to Allied Headquarters and to the American and British Governments. On March 15 General Airey and General Lemnitzer, the British and American Chiefs of Staff at Caserta, went in disguise to Switzerland, and four days later, on March 19, a second exploratory meeting was held with General Wolff.

I realised at once that the Soviet Government might be suspicious of a separate military surrender in the South, which would enable our armies to advance against reduced opposition as far as Vienna and beyond, or indeed towards the Elbe or Berlin. Moreover, as all our fronts round Germany were part of the whole Allied war the Russians would naturally be affected by anything done on any one of them. If any contacts were made with the enemy, formal or informal, they ought to be told in good time. This rule was scrupulously followed. There was at no stage any question of concealing anything from the Russians. The Allied representatives then in Switzerland even explored ways of smuggling a Russian officer in to join them if the Soviet Government wished to send someone.

On March 21 Mr. Eden accordingly instructed our Ambassador in Moscow to inform the Soviet Government of these happenings. This he did. Next day Molotov handed him a written reply, which contained the following expressions:

In Berne for two weeks, behind the backs of the Soviet Union, which is bearing the brunt of the war against Germany, negotiations have been going on between the representatives of the German military command on the one hand and representatives of the English and American commands on the other.

Sir Archibald Clark Kerr of course explained that the Soviet had misunderstood what had occurred and that these "negotiations" were no more than an attempt to test the credentials and authority of General Wolff. Molotov's comment was blunt and insulting. "In this instance," he wrote, "the Soviet Government sees not a misunderstanding, but something worse."

In the face of so astonishing a charge it seemed to me that silence was better than a contest in abuse, and on March 24 I minuted to Mr. Eden:

Prime Minister to Foreign Secretary 24 Mar. 45

For the moment these negotiations have dropped. They may be reopened in a far more vital area than Italy. In this military and political questions will be intertwined. The Russians may have a legitimate fear of our doing a deal in the West to hold them well back in the East. On the whole it will be well to send no reply [to Molotov] till we have checked up with Washington, to whom you should repeat the Russian message.

. . . . .

At the same time it was necessary to warn our military commanders in the West. I accordingly showed Molotov's insulting letter both to Montgomery and to Eisenhower, with whom I at this time was watching the crossing of the Rhine.

General Eisenhower was much upset, and seemed deeply stirred with anger at what he considered most unjust and unfounded charges about our good faith. He said that as a military commander he would accept the unconditional surrender of any body of enemy troops on his front, from a company to the entire Army, that he regarded this as a purely military matter, and that he had full authority to accept such a surrender without asking anybody's opinion. If however political matters arose he would immediately consult the Governments. He feared that if the Russians were brought into a question of the surrender of Kesselring's forces what could be settled by himself in an hour might be prolonged for three or four weeks, with heavy losses to our troops. He made it clear that he would insist upon all the troops under the officer making the surrender laying down their arms and standing still until they received further orders, so that there would be no possibility of their being transferred across Germany to withstand the Russians. He would also at the same time advance through these surrendered troops as fast as possible to the East.

I thought myself that these matters should be left to his discretion, and that the Governments should only intervene if any political issues arose. I did not see why we should break our hearts if, owing to mass surrender in the West, we got to the Elbe, or even farther, before Stalin. Jock Colville reminds me that I said to him that evening, "I hardly like to consider dismembering Germany until my doubts about Russia's intentions have been cleared away."

I minuted to Mr. Eden on March 25:

Prime Minister to Foreign Secretary 20 Mar. 45

Further reflection convinces me we should send no answer to the insulting letter from Molotov. I presume you have already sent a copy of it to the State Department, pointing out, in no spirit of complaint, that it was they who particularly wished that the Russians should not come to Switzerland and that Alexander should deal with the matter on a purely military basis. I am sure the right thing now is to get absolutely in line with the United States, which should be easy, and meanwhile let Molotov and his master wait.

I agree with you that the whole question of the San Francisco Conference hangs in the balance. The sending of Gromyko instead of Molotov is a grimace. I should suppose the President would be much offended by this.

We have had a jolly day, having crossed the Rhine. Tomorrow we go to the 15th Scottish Division, on the other side. I should think it not at all unlikely that the whole German front in the West may collapse and be broken up into blobs. There is still hard fighting going on in the North, and the brunt again seems to come from the left-hand hinge, which, as usual, we form.

And later on the same day:

Prime Minister to Foreign Secretary 25 Mar. 45

. . . We should ask the United States where they stand and whether they will now agree to a telegram from the President and me to Stalin, and secondly whether this should, as you say, cover other topics—e.g., access to Poland, treatment of our prisoners, imputations against our good faith about Berne, Rumania, etc.

Molotov's refusal to go to San Francisco is no doubt the expression of the Soviet displeasure. We should put it to Roosevelt that the whole question of going to San Francisco in these conditions is called in question and that quite definite forming up by Britain and the United States against breach of Yalta understandings now is necessary if such a meeting is to have any value.

However, I must say that we cannot press the case against Russia beyond where we can carry the United States. Nothing is more likely to bring them into line with us than any idea of the San Francisco Conference being imperilled. Could you let me have a draft on the above lines on which I can send you back a personal [message] to Roosevelt this time tomorrow? Meanwhile no answer should be sent to any of the Russian messages, even though the loss of time be prejudicial to us. When we come back at them now it must be both together. These matters will not be ripe for debate before Easter.

We have had a glorious day here, and I hope the consequences will be far-reaching. I am to see Eisenhower tomorrow at his request. I showed Montgomery Molotov's rude message, as of course the venue of the negotiations may easily be changed to his theatre. I well understand the Russian anxiety lest we should accept a military surrender in the West or South, which means that our armies will advance against little or no opposition and will reach the Elbe, or even Berlin, before the Bear. Therefore, should military negotiations break out on this front, which is not a secondary front like Italy, it will not be possible to keep the military and the political aspects separate. In my view the Russians should be in from the start, and we should carry on in accordance with our duty, our obvious advantage, and our plain right. They are claiming to have everything yielded to them at every point, and give nothing in return except their military pressure, which has never yet been exerted except in their own interest. They ought to be made to feel that we also have our point of view. In my opinion, the military, in the event of disagreement in negotiations, must refer to their Governments before reaching any conclusion.

My wife was at this time about to visit the Soviet Union on behalf of her "Aid to Russia" fund, but so intense was the Russian suspicion about the conversations at Berne that I even considered postponing her departure.

Prime Minister to Foreign Secretary 25 Mar. 45

My immediately preceding minute. I suppose it is all right Clemmie going on her journey in these circumstances. Let me know your unprejudiced opinion whether it would be better to put it off for a few days or weeks, or whether it would be considered as a sign of personal goodwill. I incline to her going as arranged.

In fact she went, and was received with the utmost goodwill. Meanwhile I carefully watched the progress of the negotiations to make sure the Soviets suffered no unfair exclusion.

Prime Minister to Foreign Secretary 30 Mar. 45

Have we not told the Russians that the only purpose of the contacts in Switzerland is to arrange a meeting at our military headquarters in Italy, where military questions will be discussed in the presence, if they wish, of a Russian representative, and that if at any moment political affairs are trenched upon the whole matter can be referred to the three Governments? It looks as if the Swiss conversations may go beyond that, if indeed they have not already gone beyond it. We have decided to ignore the insulting telegrams which Molotov has sent. This however does not relieve us from our obligation as Allies on any matter which might involve peace negotiations.

Pray consider this and let me know whether any further information should be conveyed.

. . . .

On April 5 I received from the President the startling text of his interchanges with Stalin. These were the telegrams:

Marshal Stalin to President Roosevelt 3 Apr. 45

I have received your message on the question of negotiations in Berne. You are absolutely right that, in connection with the affair regarding negotiations of the Anglo-American command with the German command somewhere in Berne or some other place, there "has developed an atmosphere of fear and distrust deserving regrets."

You insist that there have been no negotiations yet.

It may be assumed that you have not yet been fully informed. As regards my military colleagues, they, on the basis of data which they have on hand, do not have any doubts that the negotiations have taken place, and that they have ended in an agreement with the Germans, on the basis of which the German commander on the Western Front, Marshal Kesselring, has agreed to open the front and permit the Anglo-American troops to advance to the east, and the Anglo-Americans have promised in return to ease for the Germans the peace terms.

I think that my colleagues are close to the truth. Otherwise one could not have understood the fact that the Anglo-Americans have refused to admit to Berne representatives of the Soviet command for participation in the negotiations with the Germans.

I also cannot understand the silence of the British, who have allowed you to correspond with me on this unpleasant matter, and they themselves remain silent, although it is known that the initiative in this whole affair with the negotiations in Berne belongs to the British.

I understand that there are certain advantages for the Anglo-American troops as a result of these separate negotiations in Berne or some other place, since the Anglo-American troops get the possibility to advance into the heart of Germany almost without resistance on the part of the Germans, but why was it necessary to conceal this from the Russians, and why were your Allies, the Russians, not notified?

As a result of this at the present moment the Germans on the Western Front in fact have ceased the war against England and the United States. At the same time the Germans continue the war with Russia, the Ally of England and the United States. It is understandable that such a situation can in no way serve the cause of preservation of the strengthening of trust between our countries.

I have already written to you in my previous message, and consider it necessary to repeat it here, that I personally and my colleagues would never have made such a risky step, being aware that a momentary advantage, no matter what it would be, is fading before the principal advantage of the preservation and strengthening of the trust among the Allies.

This accusation angered the President deeply. His strength did not allow him to draft his own reply. General Marshall framed the following answer, with Roosevelt's approval. It certainly did not lack vigour.

President Roosevelt to Marshal Stalin 5 Apr. 45

I have received with astonishment your message of April 3 containing an allegation that arrangements which were made between Field-Marshal Alexander and Kesselring at Berne "permitted the Anglo-American troops to advance to the east, and the Anglo-Americans promised in return to ease for the Germans the peace terms."

In my previous messages to you in regard to the attempts made in Berne to arrange a conference to discuss a surrender of the German Army in Italy I have told you that (i) no negotiations were held in Berne; (ii) that the meeting had no political implications whatever; (iii) that in any surrender of the enemy Army in Italy there could be no violation of our agreed principle of unconditional surrender; (iv) that Soviet officers would be welcomed at any meeting that might be arranged to discuss surrender.

For the advantage of our common war effort against Germany, which today gives excellent promise of an early success in a disintegration of the German armies, I must continue to assume that you have the same high confidence in my truthfulness and reliability that I have always had in yours.

I have also a full appreciation of the effect your gallant Army has had in making possible a crossing of the Rhine by the forces under General Eisenhower, and the effect that your forces will have hereafter on the eventual collapse of the German resistance to our combined attacks.

I have complete confidence in General Eisenhower, and know that he certainly would inform me before entering into any agreement with the Germans. He is instructed to demand, and will demand, unconditional surrender of enemy troops that may be defeated on his front. Our advances on the Western Front are due to military action. Their speed has been attributable mainly to the terrific impact of our air-power, resulting in destruction of German communications, and to the fact that Eisenhower was able to cripple the bulk of the German forces on the Western Front while they were still west of the Rhine.

I am certain that there were no negotiations in Berne at any time, and I feel that your information to that effect must have come from German sources, which have made persistent efforts to create dissension between us in order to escape in some measure responsibility for their war crimes. If that was Wolff's purpose in Berne your message proves that he has had some success.

With a confidence in your belief in my personal reliability and in my determination to bring about together with you an unconditional surrender of the Nazis, it is astonishing that a belief seems to have reached the Soviet Government that I have entered into an agreement with the enemy without first obtaining your full agreement.

Finally I would say this: it would be one of the great tragedies of history if at the very moment of the victory now within our grasp such distrust, such lack of faith, should prejudice the entire undertaking after the colossal losses of life, material, and treasure involved.

Frankly, I cannot avoid a feeling of bitter resentment toward your informers, whoever they are, for such vile misrepresentations of my actions or those of my trusted subordinates.

I was deeply struck by this last sentence, which I print in italics. I felt that although Mr. Roosevelt did not draft the whole message he might well have added this final stroke himself. It looked like an addition or summing up, and it seemed like Roosevelt himself in anger.

I wrote at once to the President:

Prime Minister to President Roosevelt 5 Apr. 45

I am astounded that Stalin should have addressed to you a message so insulting to the honour of the United States and also of Great Britain. His Majesty's Government cordially associate themselves with your reply, and the War Cabinet have instructed me to send to Stalin the message in my immediately following. . . .

Next day I addressed Stalin myself.

Prime Minister to Marshal Stalin 6 Apr. 45

The President has sent me his correspondence with you about the contacts made in Switzerland between a British and an American officer on Field-Marshal Alexander's staff and a German general named Wolff relating to possible surrender of Kesselring's army in Northern Italy. I therefore deem it right to send you a precise summary of the action of His Majesty's Government. As soon as we learned of these contacts we immediately informed the Soviet Government on March 12, and we and the United States Government have faithfully reported to you everything that has taken place. The sole and only business mentioned or referred to in any way in Switzerland was to test the credentials of the German emissary and try to arrange a meeting between a nominee of Kesselring's with Field-Marshal Alexander at his headquarters or some convenient point in Northern Italy. There were no negotiations in Switzerland even for a military surrender of Kesselring's army. Still less did any political-military plot, as alleged in your telegram to the President, enter into our thoughts, which are not, as suggested, of so dishonourable a character.

2. Your representatives were immediately invited to the

meeting we attempted to arrange in Italy. Had it taken place and had your representatives come, they could have heard every word that passed.

3. We consider that Field-Marshal Alexander has full right to accept the surrender of the German army of twenty-five divisions on his front in Italy, and to discuss such matters with German envoys who have the power to settle the terms of capitulation. Nevertheless we took especial care to invite your representatives to this purely military discussion at his headquarters should it take place. In fact however nothing resulted from any contacts in Switzerland. Our officers returned from Switzerland without having succeeded in fixing a rendezvous in Italy for Kesselring's emissaries to come to. Of all this the Soviet Government have been fully informed step by step by Field-Marshal Alexander or by Sir Archibald Clark Kerr, as well as through United States channels. I repeat that no negotiations of any kind were entered into or even touched upon, formally or informally, in Switzerland.

4. There is however a possibility that the whole of this request to parley by the German General Wolff was one of those attempts which are made by the enemy with the object of sowing distrust between Allies. Field-Marshal Alexander made this point in a telegram sent on March 11, in which he remarks, "Please note that two of the leading figures are S.S. and Himmler men, which makes me very suspicious." This telegram was repeated to the British Ambassador in Moscow on March 12 for communication to the Soviet Government. If to sow distrust between us was the German intention it has certainly for the moment been successful.

After quoting some of the more insulting phrases from Molotov's letter I continued:

In the interests of Anglo-Russian relations His Majesty's Government decided not to make any reply to this most wounding and unfounded charge, but to ignore it. This is the reason for what you call in your message to the President "the silence of the British." We thought it better to keep silent than to respond to such a message as was sent by M. Molotov, but you may be sure that we were astonished by it and affronted that M. Molotov should impute such conduct to us. This however in no way affected our instructions to Field-Marshal Alexander to keep you fully informed.

6. Neither is it true that the initiative in this matter came, as you state to the President, wholly from the British. In fact the information given to Field-Marshal Alexander that the German General Wolff wished to make a contact in Switzerland was brought to him by an American agency.

7. There is no connection whatever between any contacts at Berne or elsewhere with the total defeat of the German armies on the Western Front. They have in fact fought with great obstinacy, and inflicted upon us and the American armies since the opening of our February offensive up to March 28 upwards of 87,000 casualties. However, being outnumbered on the ground and literally overwhelmed in the air by the vastly superior Anglo-American Air Forces, which in the month of March alone dropped over 200,000 tons of bombs on Germany, the German armies in the West have been decisively broken. The fact that they were outnumbered on the ground in the West is due to the magnificent attacks and weight of the Soviet armies.

8. With regard to the charges which you have made in your message to the President of April 3, which also asperse His Majesty's Government, I associate myself and my colleagues with the last sentence of the President's reply.

On April 7 Stalin replied to the President's reproach.

Marshal Stalin to President Roosevelt 7 Apr. 45

Your message of April 5 received.

In my message of April 3 the point at issue is not that of integrity and trustworthiness. I have never doubted your integrity and trustworthiness or Mr. Churchill's either. My point is that in the course of our correspondence it has become evident that our views differ on the point as to what is admissible and what is inadmissible as between one ally and another. We Russians think that in the present situation on the fronts, when the enemy is faced with inevitable surrender, if the representatives of any one ally ever meet the Germans to discuss surrender the representatives of another ally should be afforded an opportunity of participating in such a meeting. In any case, this is absolutely essential if the ally in question asks for such participation. The Americans and British however think differently and regard the Russian standpoint as wrong. They have, accordingly, refused the Russians the right to join in meeting the Germans in Switzerland. I have already written you, and I think it should be repeated, that in a similar situation the Russians would never have denied the Americans and British the right to join in such a meeting. I still think the Russian point of view to be the only correct one, as it precludes all possibility of mutual suspicions and makes it impossible for the enemy to sow distrust between us.

2. It is difficult to admit that the lack of resistance by the Germans on the Western Front is due solely to the fact that they have been defeated. The Germans have 147 divisions on the Eastern Front. They could without prejudicing their own position detach fifteen to twenty divisions from the Eastern Front and transfer them to reinforce their

troops on the Western Front. Yet the Germans have not done and are not doing this. They are continuing to wage a crazy struggle with the Russians for an insignificant railway station like Zemlyanitsa in Czechoslovakia, which is as much use to them as hot poultices to a corpse, and yet they yield without the slightest resistance such important towns in the centre of Germany as Osnabrück, Mannheim, and Kassel. You will agree that such behaviour on the part of the Germans is more than curious and unintelligible.

3. As regards my informants, I can assure you that they are extremely honest and modest people who discharge their duties conscientiously and have no intention of offending anyone. We have very often put these people to a practical test. Judge for yourselves. Last February General Marshall sent the Soviet General Staff a number of important reports, in which he warned the Russians, on the basis of data in his possession, that in March there would be two serious counter-attacks by the Germans on the Eastern Front—one would be aimed from Pomerania against Thorn and the other from the region of Moravska Ostrava against Lodz. In actual fact however it turned out that the Germans' main blow was being prepared and was directed not in the directions above-mentioned, but in an entirely different area, namely, in the neighbourhood of Lake Balaton, southwest of Budapest. It is common knowledge now that in this area the Germans had assembled up to thirty-five divisions, including eleven tank divisions. This was one of the heaviest attacks of the whole war, with such a large concentration of tank forces. Marshal Tolbukhin was able to avoid a catastrophe and subsequently inflict a smashing defeat on the Germans, because, among other reasons, my agents discovered, though somewhat tardily, this plan of the Germans for a major attack and immediately warned Marshal Tolbukhin. In this way I was able once again to convince my-

self how conscientious and well-informed Soviet agents are. . . .

He also sent a copy of his telegram to me, together with the following personal message:

Marshal Stalin to Prime Minister 7 Apr. 45

In my message of April 7 to the President, which I am sending to you also, I have already replied to all the fundamental points raised in your message regarding the negotiations in Switzerland. On the other questions raised in your message I consider it necessary to make the following remarks.

1. Neither I nor Molotov had any intention of "blackening" anyone. It is not a matter of wanting to "blacken" anyone, but of our having developed differing points of view as regards the rights and obligations of an ally. You will see from my message to the President that the Russian point of view on this question is the correct one, as it guarantees each ally's rights and deprives the enemy of any possibility of sowing discord between us.

2. My messages are personal and strictly confidential. This makes it possible to speak one's mind clearly and frankly. This is the advantage of confidential communications. If however you are going to regard every frank statement of mine as offensive it will make this kind of communication very difficult. I can assure you that I had and have no intention of offending anyone.

I passed this to Roosevelt, with the following comment:

Prime Minister to President Roosevelt 11 Apr. 45

I have a feeling that this is about the best we are going to get out of them, and certainly it is as near as they can get to an apology. However, before considering any answer at all from His Majesty's Government please tell me how you think the matter should be handled so that we may keep in line together.

The President answered next day that he was sending the following message to Stalin:

Thank you for your frank explanation of the Soviet point of view of the Berne incident, which now appears to have faded into the past without having accomplished any useful purpose.

There must not, in any event, be mutual distrust, and minor misunderstandings of this character should not arise in the future. I feel sure that when our armies make contact in Germany and join in a fully co-ordinated offensive the Nazis' armies will disintegrate.

And later:

President Roosevelt to Prime Minister 12 Apr. 45

I would minimise the general Soviet problem as much as possible, because these problems, in one form or another, seem to arise every day, and most of them straighten out, as in the case of the Berne meeting.

We must be firm however, and our course thus far is correct.

• 28 •

Chuck Jackson[1]

DIANA CONZETT

EVERY year at State University, the eagles in front of the Psi Gamma fraternity house were mysteriously painted during the night. Whenever this happened, it cost the Psi Gams from $75 to $100 to have the eagles cleaned. The Psi Gams complained to the University administrators, and were promised by the University president, now retired, that if ever any students were caught painting the eagles, they would be expelled from school.

On Hallowe'en, 1951, the *State News* ran a front page story about the Psi Gam eagles, stating that since the eagles had been painted on Hallowe'en past, the fraternity was expecting an "attack" again that night.

That night, Chuck Jackson, a sophomore and a member of Tri Zeta fraternity, was studying in his room, when, at about 2:30 A.M., Bill Evans, one of his fraternity brothers, came into his room and asked if Chuck

[1] Printed by permission.

would help him paint the Psi Gam eagles. He said that he needed Chuck's car to carry out the plan. Chuck agreed to do it with him, and the two boys set out. They drove past the Psi Gam house to see if anyone was watching it. They then drove by the house again, throwing bottles of paint at the eagles as they passed. They missed the eagles, hitting the house instead, and so they went back to their own house to formulate a plan which would produce more accurate results.

When they went back to the Psi Gam house again, Chuck drove the car into an alley beside the house, and held it there with the motor running. Bill approached the eagles by way of the bushes in front of the house. While waiting in the car, Chuck saw a police car drive by the front of the house. Bill also observed the car from the bushes, but assumed that they were passing on. However, the police turned down a side street, made a U turn, and came back by the house with their lights turned off. As the police drove past the Psi Gam house, Bill was in the process of breaking the paint bottles over the eagles. He ran behind the fraternity house, and climbed into the car in which Chuck was waiting. The police turned into the alley and cut off the boy's car. Chuck and Bill were taken to the Police Station where they were put in jail. The police called the Psi Gamma house, took the boys' names, and released them.

The next morning, the president of the Psi Gam house called the Dean of Students, and asked that disciplinary action be taken. The Dean then called in the Counselor to Men and the Academic Dean of the boys' college to review the case. He also called the president of the Tri Zeta house and asked him to bring the two boys down to his office the following morning.

The morning after the eagle-painting venture, Chuck met his "girl" in the student union for their daily coffee date. When he told her about the previous night's events, she asked,

"Why did you do it?"

"I was tired of studying, and it was something to do. Besides, that *News* article yesterday asked for it."

"Didn't you consider the possibility of getting caught?"

"There's always the risk element to consider, but Bill and I didn't discuss it. We wouldn't have been caught if we hadn't botched up the job."

Chuck had no idea what sort of penalty was in store for him until the next morning, just before he and Bill were to be called in by the Dean of Students. He then found out from the Counselor to Men that there was a strong possibility that the two boys would be expelled. Chuck came from a wealthy family, and had been sent away to school in the East from the time he was seven years old. He had been elected to the Cum Laude Society his junior year at prep school. His parents expected him to do well in college, and frequently reminded him that he had the ability to make Phi Beta Kappa. He knew that if he were expelled, his chances of getting into another college would be pretty slim. He expressed his feelings about the situation to his girl while waiting outside the Dean's office.

"I'm plenty tee'd off with this whole deal. It's an

awful lot to lose for a reasonably minor offense. They want to make an example of us, which is okey, but not to such an extent."

The president of Tri Zeta went into the Dean's office, and spoke in favor of the boys. He pointed out that both boys were good students, that they had never been in trouble before, and that they would be eligible for the draft if expelled.

The Dean then called the two boys into his office, and briefly told them that they had examined the facts, considered expulsion as a penalty, but decided to suspend the boys from school for a period of ten days. The boys were told that if either one was seen on the campus during the ten-day period, he would be expelled.

When Chuck came back to school after the ten day suspension period, he discussed the event with his girl once again.

"I was sure relieved that we weren't expelled," he said. "But I'm still tee'd off at him (the Dean) for handling us so summarily. Oh well, the Dean is just a big jerk."

PART V

For one word a man is often deemed to be wise and for one word he is often deemed to be foolish. We ought to be careful indeed what we say.

—Confucius

• 29 •

Key Words[1]

EDWARD W. BARRETT

EVERY experienced propagandist has learned that even while telling the same basic story world-wide, he can tell it most persuasively in each area by employing those terms that have the most meaning and appeal to the immediate audience. He soon learns that the word-concept "freedom," for example, has enormous appeal to a Filipino but is almost meaningless to a Japanese. To his amazement, he eventually learns that *there are no universally effective propaganda terms.*

So complex have the problems of semantics become to those operating in forty-six languages that one weary propaganda executive once broke up a meeting by rising, mopping his brow, and announcing, "I'm afraid I'm becoming antisemantic." Nevertheless, because official announcements must necessarily deal in words, top information officers of the government have no choice but to search continually for those word-con-

[1] From *Truth is Our Weapon,* New York, Funk & Wagnalls Company, 1953, pp. 144–148. Reprinted by permission.

cepts with the greatest appeal to the greatest number of people. To aid in the search, I once prepared a list of 42 positive word-concepts—words like *peace, liberty, honor,* and *human dignity.* To this was added a list of 14 negative word-concepts—terms like *slavery, thought control,* and *foreign domination.* The State Department then sent the lists to its public affairs staffs in a total of 157 cities around the world. It asked the public affairs officers, who had systematically studied public opinion in their areas, to rate the terms, on a scale of 0 to 100, on the basis of their propaganda effectiveness in the immediate area.

The answers, finally compiled and analyzed in the winter of 1952–53, proved fascinating. No single key word was scored highly by all posts. *Peace* ranked highest in most of the Far East but lowest in Indonesia (where the accepted translation implies "peace at any price"). It ranked well down the line in Europe, Latin America, and the Near East—perhaps because of Soviet distortion of the term. *Liberty* stood high in many countries of Latin America and Europe but low in Japan, Hong Kong, and Indochina. *Independence* ranked second (just below *peace*) in the Far East but well down the list in Latin America.

Though there was not even near-unanimity on any word, the highest rated positive words for all areas, on the average, were *independence, freedom, education, prosperity, security, national culture, peace, liberty, justice, progress,* and *honor.* The lowest rated positive words on the average represented the concept of co-operation and mutuality: *mutual assistance, world friendship, neighborliness, brotherhood, democratic unity,* and *harmony.*

The most effective negative word, on the average, turned out to be *slave labor,* followed by *Soviet imperialism, slavery, foreign domination, Communism,* and *iron curtain.* There were wide variations, however. *Iron curtain* understandably rated high in Europe, low in the Far East. *Foreign domination* ranked first in the Far East, low in Latin America.

The precise ranking of key words by the U.S.I.S. missions in each area were as follows:

Positive Key Words
Listed by Average Rank Scores and Regions

Key Word	World Average	Europe	Latin America	Africa and Near East	Far East
Independence	74	67	62	83	88
Freedom	71	71	71	71	79
Education	71	67	71	76	83
Prosperity	67	71	62	64	76
Security	67	64	62	67	79
National culture	67	67	67	64	67
Peace	64	62	64	62	90
Liberty	64	62	71	64	71
Justice	64	64	64	67	60
Progress	64	57	67	74	60
Honor	64	60	69	67	55
Human dignity	62	62	67	64	45
Faith	62	55	62	71	45
Self-government	62	60	57	67	69
Democracy	60	57	64	57	57
National equality	57	55	57	57	69

Positive Key Words (*Continued*)
Listed by Average Rank Scores and Regions

	World Average	Europe	Latin America	Africa and Near East	Far East
Cooperation	57	57	60	57	43
Human rights	57	52	55	62	52
Truth	57	60	57	57	45
Free world	57	64	55	55	48
Racial equality	55	50	43	57	76
Common good	55	52	50	40	45
Technical assistance	55	48	57	60	52
Freedom of thought	55	57	57	50	45
Anticolonialism	52	33	45	67	69
Integrity	52	57	52	50	55
Welfare	50	60	48	40	48
Decency	50	55	57	43	43
Mutual defense	50	52	45	48	48
Well-being	48	52	48	48	45
Mutual assistance	48	48	43	55	40
Humanity	45	52	43	40	38
Godliness	45	38	43	57	36
World friendship	45	48	43	45	45
Antislavery	43	45	40	45	38
Democratic strength	43	50	38	38	36
Neighborliness	40	45	38	36	40
Brotherhood	40	38	33	45	43
Individualism	38	45	33	40	19
Democratic unity	38	36	40	33	38
Harmony	33	33	33	31	31
Welfare state	26	36	33	29	19

Negative Key Words
Listed by Average Rank Scores and Regions

Key Word	World Average	Europe	Latin America	Africa and Near East	Far East
Slave labor	79	79	79	79	71
Slavery	71	57	79	79	64
Communism	71	71	79	71	71
Soviet imperialism	71	71	71	79	50
Foreign domination	71	71	64	86	86
Iron curtain	71	79	79	64	57
Police state	64	71	50	64	57
Kremlin puppets	57	64	57	57	64
Totalitarianism	57	64	57	57	50
(New) Colonialism	43	43	36	57	50
Big lie	43	43	50	50	29
Thought control	43	43	50	43	43
Indoctrination	36	43	29	43	36
Statism	29	29	21	29	21

That little study of word-concepts, plus the accompanying remarks submitted by public affairs officers, illustrated many points: the extraordinary persuasiveness of the phrase *slave labor* in describing conditions in Soviet-dominated countries, the unusual appeal of *education* in many areas, and the need to use simple terms, instead of cosmic concepts, in talking to simple people with limited horizons.

Most of all, it illustrated again the need for carefully

tailoring international information materials in accordance with the local tastes, customs, and concepts in each nation. That means that published material should be translated and edited in final form, not in Washington, but on the scene abroad. Even Voice of America broadcasts from the United States, if they are to be effective, must be subjected to continuing detailed criticism, guidance, and (where possible) editing by persons as close to the target audience as they can possibly be.

Any bureaucrat who thinks, as an occasional one does, that he can sit isolated in Washington and produce in final form the ideal item to persuade Indonesians, Chileans, or Finns ought to be isolated indeed—in a padded cell.

• 30 •

Do Doctors Make You Sick?[1]

ROBERT P. GOLDMAN

A MAN walked into a doctor's office in the Midwest and complained of a pain in his right side.

The doctor examined him and said: "I'm afraid we'll have to take your appendix out."

Hearing the bad news, the patient looked unhappy.

The doctor, seeing the man's reaction, hastily said: "Look, this isn't a serious operation. We make a small incision here (pointing to his own side), another here and that's about all."

• *When the doctor looked up, the patient had fainted. The "explanation" of the operation apparently was too much for him.*

That's a little story about a big subject.

It illustrates this:

Without wanting to, some doctors actually make people sick.

That doesn't mean you should stop going to—or

[1] *Parade*, Feb. 15, 1953, p. 9. Reprinted by permission.

switch—doctors. Chances are, your family doctor is good.

But medical authorities themselves recognize that, occasionally, an illness can be traced—*to a doctor.*

A Chance Remark

Says Dr. Franklin G. Ebaugh, clinical professor of psychiatry at the University of Colorado Medical School:

Such disorders, "unwittingly induced in the patient by the physician, are based on the physician's examination, manner and discussion."

When you analyze that statement, you realize:

• The way a doctor talks to a patient, the way he looks, the expression on his face—all may give a patient the idea that he is very sick.

Take this case:

• A man lying in a bed in a big Eastern hospital was recovering from a serious sickness. A nurse came into his room with his lunch and said, "Here, you'd better eat this—*while you can.*"

• *That chance remark left the patient thinking he was at death's door. He promptly felt worse than ever.*

Or, take another case. A woman went to a New York doctor. He examined her and said: "I'm worried about you. Do you know a good cancer specialist? You'd better see one."

Of course, the woman, her husband and son became frantic. She got depressed, as any woman would.

For another two weeks, the woman despaired.

• Finally, she went to one of the nation's top cancer

specialists. He examined her and declared: "There is no evidence that you have cancer."

• But for those two anxious weeks—*that woman was convinced that she was very sick.*

Actually, what medical specialists call "iatrogenicity," doctor-induced illness, pops up every so often in many fields of medicine.

Possibly, the most common fields are heart, cancer, stomach, and the respiratory tract.

Three New York physicians, Drs. Leonard J. Goldwater, Lewis H. Bronstein and Beatrice Kresge, writing in the Journal of the American Medical Assn., point out:

"Unwarranted" diagnosis of heart disease is sometimes made when a patient has suspicious symptoms.

On the basis of this "misdiagnosis," some of these patients are advised to limit their physical activities.

When that happens, the result is tragic—first, because the person (who doesn't really have heart trouble) is needlessly disabled; and second, because his emotions are shattered.

• Dr. Goldwater, professor of industrial hygiene at the Columbia University Public Health School, points out (and other medical authorities agree): Some patients misinterpret what the doctor tells them. They read into his statements something that isn't there.

• They "look" for trouble. So no matter what the doctor says, they feel they're sick.

But where doctors are clearly at fault, says Dr. Ebaugh, this is frequently the picture:

The doctor refuses to recognize that at the bottom of

the patient's headache, backache or other pain, *there's an emotional problem.*

So he looks hard for something *physically* wrong with the patient. As a matter of fact, he looks so hard that he "convinces" the patient *there is* something physically wrong.

Writing in the Journal of the Michigan State Medical Society, Dr. Ebaugh says, . . . "The most common cause for medically-induced illness is failure to recognize the existence of emotional factors involved."

He points out common statements like these—made from doctor to patient, may make the patient *think* he's physically sick:

• "That heart murmur—not important—probably will never bother you." Or: "I don't find your condition really serious." Or: "I'm sure everything will work out all right."

• That kind of statement, under certain circumstances, can cause this kind of idea to run through the patient's mind:

• "He didn't find anything, but there must be something wrong with me physically. He didn't tell me what, so it must be serious."

What happens? According to Dr. Ebaugh, the patient, with that idea planted in his mind, starts going from doctor to doctor—*looking for a physical illness that doesn't exist.*

At this point, the patient's original emotional problem has heaped upon it the added distress of a physical illness which the patient thinks exists.

Meanwhile, the emotional disorder goes untreated.

When that happens, the patient's whole emotional state becomes worse. The endless search for a physical ailment when only an emotional one is present, does this:

Two-Edged Sword

It supplies the patient with a "reason for being sick." That reason isn't emotional, because so many patients still cling to the false idea that it's a social disgrace to have emotional problems.

The doctor, too, may actually feel this way about illnesses due to emotional disturbances.

Dr. Ebaugh maintains, therefore: "It is obvious that the doctor's own attitudes and behavior not only are powerful factors in curing, but correspondingly may provoke or perpetuate sickness." He concludes:

"The role of the physician's personality in treatment, like a sword with two edges, may cause as well as cure disease."

REMEMBER: medical experts *themselves* recognize that there's potential dynamite in what they tell patients. Most doctors are very careful, but top authorities say occasionally there are slips. When that happens, patients can come away with strange ideas *about their health.* •

• 31 •

Fanfare Canceled for Essay Winner[1]

Sponsor of Trip to Washington Says Oklahoma Bride Copied Part of Writing Submitted

WASHINGTON, Feb. 5 (AP)—A 17-year-old bride who won a national essay contest and came to Washington with considerable fanfare lost out today on what was left of her gala reception.

Mrs. Shirley Howdeshell Malone, high school senior and bride of three weeks from Muskogee, Okla., had been adjudged the winner over 17,000 other essayists of a writing contest on "What the Bill of Rights Means to Me."

A trip to Washington was part of her reward. This afternoon's schedule called for a visit with Vice President Richard M. Nixon and the recording of a broad-

[1] *The New York Times*, Feb. 6, 1953, p. 17. Reprinted by permission of the Associated Press.

cast for the "Voice of America." Then came this announcement from the contest sponsor, the National Association of Real Estate Boards:

"We regretfully advise that we learned today that a considerable part of this essay was taken from a magazine article published in 1948.

"Due to a misunderstanding, the contestant was under the impression that assembly of available material would constitute an appropriate entry in the contest. Washington appointments have been canceled."

An association official said that when the essay was read last night "parts of it sounded familiar to someone who reported it to us and a search followed."

The girl, accompanied by her mother, Mrs. W. L. Howdeshell, arrived here yesterday. She read the essay before the annual dinner of the real estate boards last night. Appointments for today included a luncheon given by Mrs. Pearl Sayre, Oklahoma Republican National Committeewoman.

Tomorrow her schedule called for a visit with Oklahoma members of Congress and an appearance on a television program.

Oklahoma legislators challenged tonight the action of the real estate group. Representative Ed Edmondson said the contest rules had "no provision whatever concerning originality or barring the use of material from other sources" in essays submitted by the contestants.

Commenting on this statement, Edwin L. Stoll, a public relations official of the association, said:

"There's no specific statement in the contest rules saying the essays had to be original. But in a contest like that it is naturally assumed that the essayist would write their own essays and that they would be original.

"The whole thing is highly embarrassing for everyone concerned."

Rallying behind Mrs. Malone, members of the Oklahoma Congression delegation said they were going ahead with plans to give her a gala luncheon tomorrow. Senator Robert S. Kerr said:

"As I understand the situation, she won the contest fair, square and according to the rules. As far as I am concerned, I was in her corner yesterday and I'm still in her corner today."

• 32 •

"Take a Pencil . . ."[1]

THE EDITORS OF *TIME*

"THERE is great goodness in the world," Msgr. Fulton J. Sheen told an Associated Press interviewer, "but it is unsung and unheralded. To get into the papers these days, all you have to do is break one of the Ten Commandments."

Like many another churchman, Msgr. Sheen was convinced that the press gives a false picture of U.S. life by overplaying crime, lust, and violence, "prints mainly the bad, seldom the good." Said he: "Take a pencil and go through the papers. On virtually every article you can put a number . . . [to] represent a broken Commandment, the breaking of which has made news . . ."

When the Sheen story came in over the wire last week, Editor John G. Green of the Portsmouth (Ohio) *Times* (circ. 25,176) did as suggested; he took out his pencil and went through his previous day's paper. In

[1] *Time*, April 23, 1951, p. 79. Reprinted by permission. Courtesy of *Time*, copyright Time, Inc. 1951.

the 1,430 inches of news, headlines and pictures, he found only 149 inches devoted to crime or violence. Even this included stories (*e.g.*, the Korean war, the Kefauver investigation) which Editor Green thought "might be considered by many readers as being moral, rather than immoral." In the noncrime news, he counted stories about penicillin, a union convention, a parent-teachers' radio forum, a district-school music contest, new city sidewalks.

Next day, the Kansas City *Star* (circ. 364,315), which also ran the Sheen interview, did a similar job of checking up. It counted 1,535 inches of news, found only 157 inches devoted to crime and violence.

Commented the *Times:* "We agree with Msgr. Sheen's statement that 'there is great goodness in the world,' but the record seems to refute his assertion that it is 'unsung and unheralded.' "

• 33 •

"A Lie Is Always a Lie"[1]

IGNAZIO SILONE

I REMEMBER a lively discussion one day in my catechism class between the boys who were being prepared for confirmation and the parish priest. The subject was a marionette show at which we boys had been present with the priest the day before. It was about the dramatic adventures of a child who was persecuted by the devil. At one point the child-marionette had appeared on the stage trembling with fear and, to escape the devil who was searching for him, had hidden under a bed in a corner of the stage; shortly afterwards the devil-marionette arrived and looked for him in vain. "But he *must* be here," said the devil-marionette. "I can smell him. Now I'll ask these good people in the audience." And he turned to us and asked: "My dear children, have you by any chance seen that naughty child I'm looking for, hiding anywhere?" "No, no, no," we all chorused at

[1] From *The God That Failed*, Richard Crossman (ed.), New York, Harper & Brothers, 1949, pp. 84–85. Reprinted by permission.

once, as energetically as possible. "Where is he then? I can't see him," the devil insisted. "He's left, he's gone away," we all shouted. "He's gone to Lisbon." (In our part of Italy, Lisbon is still the furthermost point of the globe, even today.) I should add that none of us, when we went to the theater, had expected to be questioned by a devil-marionette; our behavior was therefore entirely instinctive and spontaneous. And I imagine that children in any other part of the world would have reacted in the same way. But our parish priest, a most worthy, cultured, and pious person, was not altogether pleased. We had told a lie, he warned us with a worried look. We had told it for good ends, of course, but still it remained a lie. One must never tell lies. "Not even to the devil?" we asked in surprise. "A lie is always a sin," the priest replied. "Even to the magistrate?" asked one of the boys. The priest rebuked him severely. "I'm here to teach you Christian doctrine and not to talk nonsense. What happens outside the Church is no concern of mine." And he began to explain the doctrine about truth and lies in general in the most eloquent language. But that day the question of lies *in general* was of no interest to us children; we wanted to know, "Ought we to have told the devil where the child was hiding, yes or no?" "That's not the point," the poor priest kept repeating to us rather uneasily. "A lie is always a lie. It might be a big sin, a medium sin, an average sort of sin, or a little tiny sin, but it's always a sin. Truth must be honored."

"The truth is," we said, "that there was the devil on one side and the child on the other. We wanted to help the child, that's the real truth." "But you've told a lie," the parish priest kept on repeating. "For good ends, I know, but still a lie." To end it, I put forward an objection of unheard-of perfidy, and, considering my age, considerable precocity: "If it'd been a priest instead of a child," I asked, "what ought we to have replied to the devil?" The parish priest blushed, avoided a reply, and, as a punishment for my impertinence, made me spend the rest of the lesson on my knees beside him. "Are you sorry?" he asked me at the end of the lesson. "Of course," I replied. "If the devil asks me for your address, I'll give it to him at once."

• 34 •

The Third Event[1]

ARMY PEARL HARBOR BOARD

8. Failure of Aircraft Warning Service to Advise of Approaching Planes, 7 December 1941.

The third event that might have saved the day was the following:

The aircraft warning service had established mobile aircraft warning stations on the Island of Oahu, as elsewhere related in detail, and had set up an Information Center to utilize the aircraft warning information, plot the course of any incoming planes, and to advise the responsible authorities. The organization was set up and operating and was being utilized from 4 A.M. to 7 o'clock on the morning of 7th December as a training method and had been so used for some time past. The Navy was supposed to have detailed officers in the Information Center to be trained as liaison officers, but had not yet gotten around to it. In the Information

[1] From the report as published in *Army and Navy Journal*, Sept. 15, 1945, pp. 94–95.

Center that morning was a Lieutenant Kermit A. Tyler, a pursuit officer of the Air Corps, whose tour of duty thereat was until 8 o'clock. It was Tyler's second tour of duty at the Center and he was there for training and observation, but there were no others on duty after 7 o'clock except the enlisted telephone operator. He was the sole officer there between 7 and 8 o'clock that morning, the rest of the personnel that had made the Center operative from 4:00 to 7:00 had departed.

At one of the remote aircraft warning stations there were two privates who had been on duty from 4 A.M. to 7 A.M. One of them was Private Lockard, who was skilled in operating the radar aircraft detector, and a Private George E. Elliott, who was the plotting man to plot the information picked up on the radar. This plotter was anxious to learn how to operate the radar, and Private Lockard agreed to show him after the station was supposed to close at 7 o'clock and while they were waiting for the truck to take them to breakfast. He kept the radar open for further operation to instruct his partner, Private Elliott. While Lockard was adjusting the machine to begin the instruction of Private Elliott, he observed on the radar screen an unusual formation he had never seen in the machine. He thought there was something wrong with it, as the indicator showed such a large number of planes coming in that he was sure that there was nothing like it in the air and there must be a machine error. He continued to check, however, and finally concluded that the machine was operating correctly and that there was a considerable number of planes 132 miles away from the island approaching from a direction 3 degrees east of north. The time was 7:02 A.M., 7 December 1941.

In this record Private Elliott, now Sergeant Elliott, testified that he plotted these planes and suggested to Lockard that they call up the Information Center. After some debate between them, Lockard did call the Information Center and reported to the switchboard operator. The switchboard operator, an enlisted man who testified, was unable to do anything about it, so he put Lieutenant Tyler on the phone. Tyler's answer proved to be a disastrous one. He said, in substance, "Forget it." Tyler's position is indefensible in his action, for he says that he was merely there for training and had no knowledge upon which to base any action; yet he assumed to give directions instead of seeking someone competent to make a decision.

If that be a fact, and it seems to be true, then he should not have assumed to tell these two men, Private Lockard and Private Elliott, to "forget it," because he did not have the knowledge upon which to premise any judgment. (R. 1102.) He should, in accordance with customary practice, have then used initiative to take this matter up with somebody who did know about it, in view of the fact that he said he was there merely for training and had no competent knowledge upon which to either tell the men to forget it or to take action upon it. By his assumption of authority, he took responsibility, and the consequences of his action should be imposed upon him.

If Tyler had communicated this information, the

losses might have been very greatly lessened. As General Short testified:

"If he had alerted the Interceptor Command there would have been time, if the pursuit squadrons had been alerted, to disperse the planes. There would not have been time to get them in the air. . . . It would have been a question of split seconds instead of minutes in getting into action." (R. 312–313.)

The attack actually took place at 7:55 A.M.

When the information that showed up on the oscilloscope was communicated, apparently Lieutenant Tyler had in his mind that a flight of B-17s was coming from the mainland and he thought that they might represent what was seen on the screen of the radar machine. As a matter of fact, that probably had something to do with it, as they did come in about this period and were attacked by the Japanese, some of them being destroyed.

• 35 •

The Use of the Word "Free"[1]

FEDERAL TRADE COMMISSION

By a 3-to-1 vote the Federal Trade Commission has ruled that the word "free" as used in Book-of-the-Month Club advertisements and promotional literature is "false, misleading, and deceptive."

Accordingly, the Commission issued an order directing Book-of-the-Month Club, Inc., 385 Madison Ave., New York, and its officers, agents, and representatives to stop:

"Using the word 'free,' or any other word or words of similar import or meaning, in advertising to designate or describe any book, or other merchandise, which is not in truth and in fact a gift or gratuity or is not given to the recipient thereof without requiring the purchase of other merchandise or requiring the performance of some service inuring, directly or indirectly, to the benefit of the respondent."

In support of the Commission's findings of fact and

[1] From the press release, Friday, May 16, 1952.

order, Chairman James M. Mead filed a majority opinion which was concurred in by Commissioners John Carson and Stephen J. Spingarn. Commission Lowell B. Mason filed a dissenting opinion. . . .

The Commission's findings include a typical advertisement in which "A FREE Copy" of a designated book is offered "To New Members of the Book-of-the-Month Club." The ad contains a membership enrollment coupon which reads:

"Please enroll me as a member. I am to receive, free, [the designated book] with the purchase of my first book indicated below, and thereafter for every two books-of-the-month I purchase from the Club, I am to receive, free, the current book-dividend then being distributed. I agree to purchase at least four books-of-the-month—or special members' editions—from the Club each full year I am a member, and I may cancel my subscription any time after purchasing four such books from the Club."

Another excerpt from the ad says that "Last year the retail value of the free books Club members received was in excess of $16,000,000—books given to members, not sold! . . . Why not share in this distribution, particularly since you need never take any book you do not want, and actually pay less for many books?"

The use of the word "free" to describe the enrollment book, the Commission said, "has tremendous advertising value in inducing people to sign and send in the membership coupon." Actually, the findings continue, "the books designated as 'free' are not gifts or gratuities or without cost to the recipient but, on the contrary, the prospective member, before he is entitled to receive such books, must join the Book-of-the-Month Club and assume the obligation to purchase at least four books from respondent over the period of a year, the fulfillment of which obligation inures directly to the profit of the respondent."

As additional evidence that the books are not free, the Commission pointed out that if a member does not purchase at least four books from the Club within a year of his application for membership, "payment for the book theretofore designated as 'free' is thereafter demanded by the respondent."

The Commission said the Club's advertisements have deceived members of the purchasing public into the erroneous and mistaken belief "that books offered as 'free to new members' are given without charge or obligation. . . ."

One of the allegations of the complaint in the proceeding was that the Club's use of the term "book-dividends" in advertising was false and misleading. The Commission ruled that this charge was not sustained by the evidence.

The complaint was dismissed as to Harry Scherman and Meredith Wood as individuals but not in their capacities as officers of Book-of-the-Month Club, Inc.

Three other complaints involving alleged misuse of the word "free" in advertising books are pending before the Commission. . . .

Order Dismissing Complaint[2]

FEDERAL TRADE COMMISSION

THE Federal Trade Commission has ruled that goods given without cost upon the purchase of other merchandise may be described as "free." But it made clear that the term must be used "honestly" and not as a "device for deceiving the public."

In permitting use of the word "free" to describe gifts contingent on the purchase of other merchandise, the Commission reversed a policy in effect since January 1948.

Under the new ruling, use of such terms as "free" in advertising or in other offers to the public will be considered "unfair or deceptive" under these circumstances:

1. When all of the conditions, obligations or other prerequisites to the receipt and retention of the "free" article of merchandise are not clearly and conspicuously explained or set forth at the outset so as to leave no reasonable probability that the terms of the advertisement or offer might be misunderstood; or

2. When, with respect to the article of merchandise required to be purchased in order to obtain the "free" article, the offerer either (1) increases the ordinary and usual price; or (2) reduces the quality; or (3) reduces the quantity or size of such article of merchandise.

[2] From the press release, Friday, September 18, 1953.

Under the former policy, the Commission had prohibited the use of the word "free" to describe merchandise to which any strings were attached. To be called "free," the merchandise had to be "in truth and in fact a gift or gratuity"—given without requiring the purchase of other merchandise or the performance of any service inuring directly or indirectly to the benefit of the advertiser or seller.

The change of policy was signalled in two separate actions:

1. The Commission rescinded its "administrative interpretation" respecting use of the word "free," as published in the *Federal Register* of January 30, 1948.

2. The Commission dismissed its complaint against Walter J. Black, Inc., trading as The Classics Club and Detective Book Club, New York, charging it with violation of the Federal Trade Commission Act in connection with its "free" offers of books to new members of the clubs.

It was in the majority opinion in this case that the Commission outlined its new position stressing that it will proceed against use of the term only where the circumstances result in a tendency or capacity to mislead or deceive the public.

The opinion was written by Commissioner Albert A. Carretta and concurred in by Chairman Edward F. Howrey and Commissioner Lowell B. Mason.

Commissioners James M. Mead and Stephen J. Spingarn concurred in the decision to dismiss the Black case but dissented in part from the views expressed in the majority opinion. Commissioner Mead said he will file a separate opinion later.

Commissioner Spingarn also dissented from the Commission's action in rescinding the policy statement of January 14, 1948. Commissioner Mead did not participate in this decision because of absence.

In the Black case, the company offered books "free" to new members.

Before August 1951, according to the majority opinion, an enrollee in the Detective Book Club, upon accepting the free book or books, obligated himself to purchase additional books during the ensuing twelve months.

With regard to The Classics Club, however, the Commission said that, "there is no evidence in the record to indicate that the respondent ever required enrollees in The Classics Club to purchase any specific number of books in order to obtain a 'free' book or books."

Concerning the current advertising of both The Classics Club and the Detective Book Club, the Commission said that enrollees are not obligated to take any specific number of books and may reject any book before or after receipt.

The majority opinion made clear, however, that the fact recipients of the "free" books were not actually required to purchase other books was not the basis of the dismissal order. Even had there been an obligation to purchase other books, the practice would have been within the new ruling so long as the obligation was "clearly and conspicuously explained" at the outset and so long as the article of merchandise required to be purchased remained unchanged as to price, quality, and quantity.

Accordingly, the Commission reversed the initial decision of the hearing examiner and ruled that the advertising of the Black corporation was not unfair or deceptive as charged.

The majority opinion emphasizes that the Commission will continue to proceed against deceptive use of the word "free." The opinion said:

> . . . there must be truth in advertising to support the use of the word "free." If an advertiser either lies as to the facts or tells only part of the truth in his advertising, and such lies or omissions have the tendency or capacity to mislead or deceive the public, this Commission, pursuant to the authority delegated to it by Congress, must inhibit such use of the word "free" in advertising. . . .

PART VI

Some to the fascination of a name,
Surrender judgment hoodwink'd.
—William Cooper

• 36 •

Do You Speak American?[1]

ASHLEY HALSEY, JR.

IF A certain long, slim insect with two pairs of wings were to fly cross-country from Maine to Georgia, people noticing it flit by would call it a "devil's darning needle" in New England, a "spindle" in parts of New Jersey, a "dragonfly" in most cities, a "snake waiter" in the Pennsylvania-German country, a "snake feeder" in the Appalachians, and a "snake doctor" or "mosquito hawk" elsewhere down South.

These seven local names for a single commonplace insect were noted by researchers for the *Linguistic Atlas of the United States*, a scholarly record of the surprising variations in America's spoken language. The fact that a flying insect can travel under seven aliases pales beside some other things the researchers have turned up.

Millions of Americans, for example, will squirm with embarrassment if you ask to hang your clothes in their "closet." "Closet" still means a backyard convenience to them. "Evening" is any time after 12:30 P.M. in

[1] "Report to the Editors," *The Saturday Evening Post*, June 10, 1950. Reprinted by permission of the author and editor.

Southern rural areas, often to the confusion of city folks who arrive hours late when invited to an "evening" meal. A Tennessean who refers to his "harp" isn't being coyly angelic—he means his "mouth harp" or mouth organ.

Dr. Guy Lowman, Jr., one of the chief field workers, once asked a Virginia farm wife whether her husband kept a "bull." Her grown son, flushing at what he regarded as a frightful insult to his mother, chased Doctor Lowman out of the house. Since then, the researchers have learned that many farmers studiously avoid using "bull," "stud," "ram," and "boar" around their womenfolk. Some have fancy substitutes such as "he-brute" or plain "brute" in parts of North Carolina, "mean animal" or "mean critter" elsewhere on the Atlantic seaboard, and "stock cow" in upper South Carolina. The politest reference recorded made him a "gentleman cow," and one of the most cynical, cited by H. L. Mencken, had him a "preacher cow."

Similarly, residents of rural areas lean over backward to avoid saying "outhouse." The project reveals the use of approximately 500 substitute expressions by actual count. At least one of the terms, reports Dr. Raven I. McDavid, Jr., resulted from anything but a desire to be polite. In a Georgia hill area which felt slighted by the state government, a favorite term for outhouse is "state capitol."

The atlas project, sponsored by the American Council of Learned Societies and headed by Dr. Hans Kurath, of the University of Michigan, is intended primarily to record all the ramifications of American speech before radio, television, and other nationwide influences blur sectional and local usages. A rural tendency to copy the speech of big-city people has already been noted in some sections.

Aside from its value to scholars, the atlas is expected to prove helpful in many ways. Mail-order businesses may use it to avoid the confusion caused by such things as the upstate New York habit of calling a tin gutter an "eaves trough"—and ordering accordingly. Amnesia victims may be aided in locating their homes by word tests such as "greasy." If pronounced "gree-sy," to rhyme with "fleecy," the speaker was born north of an imaginary cross-country line just above Philadelphia. Otherwise, he pronounces "greasy" like "easy."

The atlas came in unexpectedly handy when the father of a University of Michigan researcher, a farmer in Michigan's "Thumb" section, bought a carload of Ohio sheep. After trying for days to herd them with the usual call, "KO-day, KO-day!" the farmer wrote his son despondently, "These are the dumbest sheep. I yell myself hoarse and they never turn their heads." The son, checking atlas findings, learned that "KO-day" was a call brought West by New England settlers, whereas Ohio was settled by Pennsylvanians and Southerners who simply called "Sheep!" So he wrote his father, "Just try calling 'Sheep!' " The reply is treasured by the atlas makers.

"Son," the old farmer wrote happily. "I didn't expect the University of Michigan to teach you how to call Ohio sheep. But it's done the trick. They come running."

• 37 •

Retroactive Weather[1]

JOHN CROSBY

THAT tireless investigator of other people's business, Allen Funt, took his "Candid Camera" and his concealed microphone out the other day to find out how many people knew what the word *retroactive* meant. He walked up to an elevator starter and declared belligerently: "Listen, I think you ought to know that the last elevator on the right side is retroactive."

"Gee," said the starter, "haven't heard any complaints from the elevator man."

"It's dangerous."

"Gee, we'll have to look into it. You think it's very dangerous."

"It certainly is dangerous. You can get into all kinds of trouble with that."

Mr. Funt then wandered out, smiling his sadistic smile, and accosted a young lady at a soda fountain.

[1] From the "Radio and Television" column by John Crosby in the *New York Herald Tribune* of June 29, 1950. Reprinted by permission.

"Boy," he exclaimed, "isn't this weather retroactive, though." She agreed heartily that it was.

"Most retroactive day we've had," said Funt.

"Yes," said the girl. "Terrible."

"You know what retroactive weather is, don't you?" asked Funt.

"Very hot without stopping," said the girl firmly.

The next victim was a gentleman window shopping. "Hey, buddy," said Funt grimly. "If I were you I wouldn't go into that store."

"Why not?"

"Those people in there, they're very retroactive . . . I mean if a store is retroactive, the least you can do is pass 'em by."

"Well," said the man uncertainly, "as long as you insist."

"I don't insist. It's just my advice. Would you—do you—ever go into stores that are retroactive?"

"Well, I've taken chances before."

• 38 •

The Name of the Situation as Affecting Behavior[1]

B. L. WHORF

THERE will probably be general assent to the proposition that an accepted pattern of using words is often prior to certain lines of thinking and forms of behavior, but he who assents often sees in such a statement nothing more than a platitudinous recognition of the hypnotic power of philosophical and learned terminology on the one hand or of catchwords, slogans, and rallying-cries on the other. To see only thus far is to miss the point of one of the important interconnections which Sapir saw between language, culture, and psychology. . . . It is not so much in these special uses of language as in its constant ways of arranging data and its most ordinary

[1] From "The Relation of Habitual Thought and Behavior to Language," in *Language, Culture, and Personality, Essays in Memory of Edward Sapir*, edited by Leslie Spier, A. Irving Hallowell, Stanley S. Newman, pp. 75–77. Menasha, Wisconsin, Sapir Memorial Fund, 1941. Reprinted by permission.

every-day analysis of phenomena that we need to recognize the influence it has on other activities, cultural and personal.

I came in touch with an aspect of this problem before I had studied under Dr. Sapir, and in a field usually considered remote from linguistics. It was in the course of my professional work for a fire insurance company, in which I undertook the task of analyzing many hundreds of reports of circumstances surrounding the start of fires, and in some cases, of explosions. My analysis was directed toward purely physical conditions, such as defective wiring, presence or lack of air spaces between metal flues and woodwork, etc., and the results were presented in these terms. Indeed it was undertaken with no thought that any other significances would or could be revealed. But in due course it became evident that not only a physical situation *qua* physics, but the meaning of that situation to people, was sometimes a factor, through the behavior of the people, in the start of the fire. And this factor of meaning was clearest when it was a *linguistic meaning*, residing in the name or the linguistic description commonly applied to the situation. Thus around a storage of what are called "gasoline drums" behavior will tend to a certain type, that is, great care will be exercised; while around a storage of what are called "empty gasoline drums" it will tend to be different—careless, with little repression of smoking or of tossing cigarette stubs about. Yet the "empty" drums are perhaps the more dangerous, since they contain explosive vapor. Physically the situation is hazardous, but the linguistic analysis according to regular analogy must employ the word "empty," which inevitably suggests lack of hazard. The word "empty" is used in two linguistic patterns: (1) as a virtual synonym for "null and void, negative, inert," (2) applied in analysis of physical situations without regard to, e.g., vapor, liquid vestiges, or stray rubbish, in the container. The situation is named in one pattern (2) and the name is then "acted out" or "lived up to" in another (1); this being a general formula for the linguistic conditioning of behavior into hazardous forms.

In a wood distillation plant the metal stills were insulated with a composition prepared from limestone and called at the plant "spun limestone." No attempt was made to protect this covering from excessive heat or the contact of flame. After a period of use the fire below one of the stills spread to the "limestone," which to everyone's great surprise burned vigorously. Exposure to acetic acid fumes from the stills had converted part of the limestone (calcium carbonate) to calcium acetate. This when heated in a fire decomposes, forming inflammable acetone. Behavior that tolerated fire close to the covering was induced by use of the name "limestone," which because it ends in "stone" implies noncombustibility.

A huge iron kettle of boiling varnish was observed to be overheated, nearing the temperature at which it would ignite. The operator moved it off the fire and ran it on its wheels to a distance, but did not cover it. In a minute or so the varnish ignited. Here the linguistic influence is more complex; it is due to the metaphorical objectifying (of which more later) of "cause" as contact or the spatial juxtaposition of "things"—to analyzing the situation as "on" versus "off" the fire. In reality the stage when the external fire was the main factor had passed; the overheating was now an internal process of convection in the varnish from the intensely heated kettle, and still continued when "off" the fire.

An electric glow heater on the wall was little used, and for one workman had the meaning of a convenient coat-hanger. At night a watchman entered and snapped a switch, which action he verbalized as "turning on the light." No light appeared, and this result he verbalized as "light is burned out." He could not see the glow of the heater because of the old coat hung on it. Soon the heater ignited the coat, which set fire to the building.

A tannery discharged waste water containing animal matter into an outdoor settling basin partly roofed with wood and partly open. This situation is one that ordinarily would be verbalized as "pool of water." A workman had occasion to light a blow-torch nearby, and threw his match into the water. But the decomposing waste matter was evolving gas under the wood cover, so that the setup was the reverse of "watery." An instant flare of flame ignited the woodwork, and the fire quickly spread into the adjoining building.

A drying room for hides was arranged with a blower at one end to make a current of air along the room and thence outdoors through a vent at the other end. Fire started at a hot bearing on the blower, which blew the flames directly into the hides and fanned them along the room, destroying the entire stock. This hazardous setup followed naturally from the term "blower" with its linguistic equivalence to "that which blows," implying that its function necessarily is to "blow." Also its function is verbalized as "blowing air for drying," overlooking that it can blow other things, e.g., flames and sparks. In reality a blower simply makes a current of air and can exhaust as well as blow. It should have been installed at the vent end to *draw* the air over the hides, then through the hazard (its own casing and bearings) and thence outdoors.

Beside a coal-fired melting pot for lead reclaiming was dumped a pile of "scrap lead"—a misleading verbalization, for it consisted of the lead sheets of old radio condensers, which still had paraffin paper between them. Soon the paraffin blazed up and fired the roof, half of which was burned off.

Such examples, which could be greatly multiplied, will suffice to show how the cue to a certain line of behavior is often given by the analogies of the linguistic formula in which the situation is spoken of, and by which to some degree it is analyzed, classified, and allotted its place in that world which is "to a large extent unconsciously built up on the language habits of the group." And we always assume that the linguistic analysis made by our group reflects reality better than it does.

• 39 •

Psomophagist[1]

WHITNEY J. OATES

Not long ago a very enthusiastic classicist, a lawyer by profession, was talking about the values and benefits of classical education. He said, "I have found it tremendously valuable; it puts money in my pocket. I want to tell you how it is done. A client of mine, who was arrested for drunken driving and who had pleaded guilty, found himself in a position involving political complications and it became very necessary for him to be let off. Therefore, I was engaged as his attorney. I didn't know how I was going to get a man off when he had already confessed himself as guilty. So I decided that I would cross-examine the doctor who had certified that my client was drunk. After the doctor took the stand I put this question to the witness, 'Doctor, what would you say if I told you that the defendant was a pso-

[1] From "Classic Theories of Communication" in *The Communication of Ideas* (ed. Lyman Bryson), New York, Harper & Brothers, 1948, pp. 28–29. Reprinted by permission.

mophagist?' The doctor scratched his head and said he didn't know; it was probably pretty serious. Then I said, 'What if I should tell you, doctor, that my client is a congenital psomophagist?' The doctor shook his head, 'Pretty serious.' In the meantime, many law attendants were scrambling in the dictionary. After the doctor admitted that it was a very serious condition, I successfully moved that the case be dismissed."

The lawyer had played a simple trick. He merely made up a word from Greek roots: "psomophagist" means nothing except a person who bolts his food. It is very difficult to find in the dictionary. In the first place, it isn't there, and in the second place, it begins with "ps" instead of an "s." Clearly this anecdote illustrates a certain type of communication, and I should say that it is against this kind of thing in its ancient form in classical Greece that Plato moved with all the power of his mind and his thought.

• 40 •

Tumor Clinic, Metropolitan Hospital[1]

SEMANTICS WORKSHOP ASSOCIATES

MISS MARY GREEN, Social Welfare worker in the Out-Patient Department of the Metropolitan Hospital, was having continuing trouble with patients who had been referred to the Tumor Clinic of that hospital.

Miss Green had observed that most of the patients arrived at the Clinic after a short visit in one of the general out-patient receiving-rooms, where they were given a brief examination. Many of the patients presented themselves at the hospital's free clinic. When they arrived, they were either examined by the doctor or interne on duty and then referred to another clinic for treatment, or sometimes were directed to the appropriate clinic by the reception clerks. Miss Green had the impression that very few of the patients arriving at the

[1] Reprinted by permission. Prepared for use originally by the Boston Society for General Semantics in 1947–1948.

Tumor Clinic had been given reassurance in the short examination, or very much information about tumors and cancer which would keep them from worrying about their condition.

In reports to her superior, Miss Green included some detailed impressions which she had written down after talking with some of the patients.

"One elderly lady," read part of a report written in November, 1947, "caused considerable disturbance when she arrived here after being referred to the Tumor Clinic by the doctor in the General Clinic. She expressed vigorous resistance when asked to enter the examination-room, and was sent to me. I tried to explain to her that she had been sent here only for diagnosis, and that it was not certain whether the doctor would find anything. I stressed the fact that an early diagnosis would be of great importance if she did have something needing treatment. She finally consented to go in, but she was visibly reluctant to go. I had the feeling that she was frightened at the thought that she might have a cancer."

Other reports indicated that the patients referred to this clinic very often showed signs of anxiety, to a degree noticeably greater than patients going to other clinics.

Henry Thomas, a 55-year-old patient, told Miss Green: "I came in for a check-up and they sent me down here. I didn't have time to come that day. That night my wife asked me how the check-up had been, and I told her they sent me to the Tumor Clinic. She got all upset then, and pretty soon I got to feeling pretty bad myself. Just the idea that I may have cancer is enough to make me lose my appetite sometimes. I once used to know a man who had cancer, and for two years before he died he was in awful pain. I always said I'd rather shoot myself than die of cancer."

Miss Green was asked to see a woman of 47 who was waiting for the doctor. She found the woman in an extremely agitated state, and asked if there were anything she could do until the doctor could see her.

"No one can do anything now," the woman said. "They think I've got a cancer, and they told me to come down here. When they told me to come down here, I just knew I had cancer. They might as well tell me right out. I think they are trying to hide it from me. But on the radio the man said this bump I've got might be a cancer. I've been feeling bad anyhow, and I know I got it. When the doctor told me to come down here, I knew the worst. They don't send you here to the Clinic for nothing. The man on the radio talked about tumors and bumps, and I know that's what I got."

The woman was barely able to keep from crying when she went in to see the doctor.

Miss Green summed up one report in late November: "The patients hear the words Tumor Clinic and they become frightened. To be referred to this Clinic is to some of them equivalent to a diagnosis of incurable cancer. The great publicity given to cancer over the radio and on posters has apparently added to some of their fears."

The physicians and the surgeons of the hospital staff were aware of the problem, and repeatedly stated that they thought something should be done to combat patients' fears that all tumors were malignant and incurable. One of the resident physicians pointed out that they could not give too much optimistic encouragement, or there would be the danger that early cases would not be caught by diagnosis in time for effective treatment.

"Many patients," he said, "would take any optimistic views as sufficient warrant to stay away. Most of them are frightened by disease anyhow, and are further frightened at the thought that they might have cancer. We have to get them in here if possible. But I feel that we should keep from frightening them unnecessarily with the name of the Tumor Clinic before they have been diagnosed."

Miss Green, in discussing the problem with other coworkers and with her superior in the Welfare Department, felt that the name of the Clinic should be changed. The superior told them that the staff had considered that possibility in a recent staff meeting, but had reached no decision yet.

Miss Green's superior added that the staff had set two requirements for the new name, if that should prove to be the best way of handling the situation. The new name, she told them, would have to be innocuous to the patients, and it also had to be medically sound.

Considering these requirements, Miss Green wondered whether a new name wouldn't soon become synonymous with "cancer" and cause the same trouble as the old name. She had read a report that a New York State "Home for Incurables" had found it necessary to change its name to "Hospital for Chronic Diseases." The director of this hospital had added that if the new name proved unsatisfactory, they would change the name again.

As she talked over her evaluation of the situation with one of her co-workers, Miss Green at one point received the opinion of one of her friends: "I don't see that changing the name is the solution at all. After all, we have the right name now. If you change the name, you'll just confuse the patients. This is where the hospital handles tumor cases, and I think it's wrong to put a false name on the door."

• 41 •

The Democratic Party[1]

GRETCHEN FINLETTER

CERTAIN principles are confused in the mind of a child. Grown-up people are busy; but unless issues are properly explained, great walls of misunderstanding can arise. Children are loyal; and if their parents feel deeply about some cause, they will feel deeply also, though often they haven't the faintest idea what it is about.

When I was very little, I felt that there was something wrong about being a Democrat. I didn't know what a Democrat was, where he fitted in—I wasn't even sure he was an American—but I did know he was an outcast. I knew that my mother was the daughter of James G. Blaine, a great Republican, and that that was something to be very proud of. I had heard my mother and my aunt talk over campaigns and elections where his leadership had been challenged. Even when I was very small I knew the bitter feelings that can arise in political life.

One summer day my cousin Walker and I—we were

[1] From *From The Top of The Stairs*, by Gretchen Finletter, by permission of Little, Brown & Co., and the Atlantic Monthly Press, pp. 106–109. Copyright 1943, 1944, 1945, 1946 by Gretchen Finletter.

about five years old—were walking through the woods at Bar Harbor. We were considering adventuring on a new path where with luck we might get lost. As we debated this possibility, we saw coming toward us a young man in white flannels—Amos Pinchot. We told him of our problem. He was sympathetic and pointed out a new path that he would take us on some day, and where he promised us we should be well lost. Then he pulled out of his pocket two buttons and pinned them on our chests.

"Wear these and your mothers will do what you ask," he told us.

"Anything?"

"Anything," he promised us.

On each button was the face of an eagle-eyed man with hair that curled over his collar. Underneath the face were some letters, but we did not know how to read.

We wore our buttons hopefully in to lunch, eager to see how soon their magic would begin. My aunt was the first to notice them.

"What have you got on?" she asked.

"Mr. Pinchot gave them to us," I told her proudly.

My aunt started to laugh. "Margaret, look. They're Bryan buttons!"

My mother did not take it so lightly. "Get rid of them immediately!" she cried. "No one can wear a Bryan button in this house. Destroy them!"

Walker and I bolted upstairs to the bathroom, where we disposed of the buttons. Walker was more informed than I. "He's a *Democrat*," he told me.

I had often heard the Democratic Party spoken of with great disapproval. To me a party meant ice cream and chocolate cake, so I assumed from the gloomy reports that when the Democrats gave their parties they were always failures. I often wondered what went wrong. Did the guests not arrive, or was it like so many parties—not quite so much fun as one had expected? The Republican parties, I gathered, were great successes. Everyone came.

When I grew a little older and did begin faintly to understand that this all referred to a political structure, the first picture was so engraved on my mind that when the parties were referred to, I continued to see a lace cloth and candies and the ever-present threat that something was going to spoil the occasion. And to this day I cannot rid myself of that first impression. My mother imbued us with so strong a feeling of loyalty to the Republican Party that when I have deviated and voted the Democratic ticket, I have done so with a sense of wrong toward her, and I am still nervous about telling her.

At the last election, I confessed to her that I was going to vote for President Roosevelt. My mother told me to do what I thought was right. This gesture on her part, which was a big gesture, only increased my old sense of guilt; and as I stood in the polling booth, the same picture rose to my eyes again, of the tables covered with snappers and cakes, and I was sitting at the table where something might go wrong. I wasn't at my mother's party.

• 42 •

Alderman Peter J. McGuinness and Mayor Hylan[1]

RICHARD H. ROVERE

THE best example of McGuinness's resourcefulness as a politician is his campaign for farm gardens for the children of Greenpoint. During the first World War, most of the local war gardening was done in city parks, parts of which were plowed up and parcelled out to amateur vegetable growers. McGuinness found that the children in his district enjoyed working in the gardens, and when the war was over he persuaded the city administration to let them continue. After a few years, however, when McGuinness's skill at legislative maneuvering was getting Greenpoint far more than the district's fair share of appropriations for improvements, the Board of Estimate began to rebel. By persuasive argument, McGuinness headed off several attacks, but

[1] "Profiles, The Big Hello—II," *The New Yorker*, Jan. 19, 1946, pp. 30–32. Reprinted by permission.

finally he was forced to use guile. He got the funds that made the gardens possible by announcing that, to show the Board how much the children appreciated the privilege, he was going to bring six hundred of them to City Hall for the Board's public hearing on the matter. "I knew that would scare the bejesus out of them," he says. He told a functionary that he had chartered several buses to get the children over. "They'll need a lot of room, God bless them," he said, "because I want them to have their little shovels and hoes and rakes along with them to show the Mayor how much they love tilting the soil." The prospect of six hundred youngsters loose in City Hall with garden tools produced immediate assurance from Mayor Hylan that the appropriations would go through.

The next year, McGuinness got money for the gardens by nominating Mayor Hylan for President. He says that he argued before the Board for an hour and knew that he would lose unless he got the support of the Mayor. "I could see he was going to vote against me," he says. "The sweat was pouring down me back. All the nerves of me body was jumping. I could just see them kids when I had to tell them there wouldn't be any more gardens. Then it just came to me. It burst right into me brain. I made it up as I went along." He said:

Mr. Mayor, in the history of our glorious country there have been two great Presidents. One was the Honorable George Washington, who led this nation to freedom, and the other was the Honorable Abraham Lincoln, who freed the poor slaves in 1865. Ever since 1865 a pair of old black shoes have been standing beside the President's desk in the

White House. Those shoes are old and worn, but they stay there in the White House because they know that the man who used to walk around in them was loved in the hearts of the poor people of America. And he loved the poor people, too, Mr. Mayor. He was the man who said that God must have loved the poor people because he made so many of them. Now, when they laid Abraham Lincoln away, those shoes came walking back into the White House and put themselves beside his desk, and they've been waiting there ever since for a man who loves the poor people as much as he did to come in and fill them. Today, Mr. Mayor, the City of New York is going to fill those shoes with one of its own, John Francis Hylan, who in his splendid wisdom in voting for these farm gardens is bringing happiness into the lives of the little ones of Greenpoint and is showing his people and the great Democratic Party, which has always fought for the poor people, that he loves them too. John Francis Hylan will be the next President of the United States.

Hylan cast his three votes for the appropriations. The next morning the newspapers ran stories headlined "Hylan-for-President Move Started by Local Democratic Leader" and the like. When reporters called on McGuinness, he ducked most of their questions. "Hylan's a splendid man," he said, "one of the highest-type men in the country today." When he was finally pinned down, however, he said, "What the hell, I don't mind giving out a few nominations if it will help Greenpoint."

PART VII

My bane and antidote are both before me.
—Joseph Addison

• 43 •

How to Argue[1]

STUART CHASE

SUPPOSE a stranger tries to pick a quarrel with you, at a cocktail party, let us say, or a conference. He comes up and says: "I hear you like labor unions; well, they are nothing but a lot of rackets!"

Suppose further that you have a long and honorable record as an impartial student of labor problems, which makes this pretty close to an insult. What are you going to do?

There are three obvious things to do—and one not so obvious. You can hit him. You can turn your back and walk away with as much dignity as you can summon. You can say: "You don't know what you're talking about!" and start a slam-bang argument. This will probably draw a crowd like a soapbox debate, and like such debates it will get precisely nowhere.

[1] *Reader's Digest*, November 1952, pp. 25–26. Reprinted by permission.

These are the normal courses of action, but this time, in the interests of peace, and of science, suppose you try an experiment. Stand your ground, put on as reasonable an expression as can be mustered, and say nothing at all.

Your man looks surprised, but soon rallies to the attack: "Pegler is dead right when he says unions are all run by racketeers!"

You continue to keep your foot hard on the brake. The essence of the experiment is to refuse to argue on big general statements, where nobody knows what the other fellow means. "Well," you say, "that's one point of view. Tell me some more."

Your man blinks and clears his throat. He is plainly disconcerted. "Well—er—Pegler ought to know, oughtn't he?" Now he is moving from offensive to defensive. If you are tempted to follow up the advantage, resist the temptation.

"Go ahead," you say, "I'm listening." And you *are* listening. You are trying to determine what makes him act this way. Did a labor union once give him a rough deal? Or what?

Your man opens his mouth, closes it, and goes into neutral. "Well, some people think they're rackets; what do you think?" This is the signal that the experiment has been successful! The attack has fizzled out. The man who came to back you into a corner is now asking your opinion. You can leave him disarmed, or you can continue the experiment. Suppose you tell him about a case of racketeering which you personally investigated. "A very bad business." (You have saved his face by admitting he has a case; some unions are indeed rackets.) "But now take the Amalgamated Clothing Workers, who even endorse bank loans sometimes to employers who are in trouble. One could hardly call that racketeering?"

Since you have listened to him, he is now willing to listen to you. He admits that the Amalgamated is a responsible union. He admits that he may be a little prejudiced. You can then discuss various other cases without emotion, on their merits. Both of you learn something which neither of you knew before. No fisticuffs, no enemies, no shouting, and no backing down on your part.

This ingenious technique was first outlined to me by S. I. Hayakawa, a social scientist in Chicago. I have used it on a number of occasions with considerable success.

The essence is in *listening*. Don't hit, don't contradict, don't cave in or turn the other cheek. Just say: "Tell me some more, I'm listening."

Bernard Shaw once said that the degree of emotion in a controversy varies inversely with knowledge of the subject. And usually the offensive does have very few facts with which to back up its emotion. (I find that most attackers run out of gas in about three minutes.)

When you accept your attacker as a human being with a legitimate point of view, his self-confidence is not threatened; he will eventually try to find out what *you* think, and may go quite a way to agree with you.

• 44 •

Listening and Disagreeing[1]

WILLIAM FOOTE WHYTE

A Full Hearing

WHEN a man states a point of view on which you disagree, there are two contrasting ways of meeting the situation:

1. You can immediately bring in counterarguments to show him that he is wrong.

2. You can express interest (not approval) in his point of view and ask him to tell you more about it. Why does he feel the way he does? What is behind his thinking?

These two moves lead in opposite directions. The first move leads to increasingly sharp disagreements, marked by briefer and more rapid interchanges, more interruptions, and rising emotional tension.

The second move leads to relaxed tension and makes agreement possible. The man does not feel under pres-

[1] From *Pattern for Industrial Peace* by William Foote Whyte, by permission of Harper & Brothers, pp. 181–184. Copyright 1951.

sure to get out his statement in a hurry and prepare for counterattack. He is able to talk to the subject and around it, in an informal, exploratory manner. You are able then to size up possibilities of getting together.

If we review the negotiation record in this case, we find many instances of this second approach. That was Shafer's way of meeting management's arguments.

For example, take the first argument over rate arbitration. Kaufman introduced the subject, suggested that the union speak first on it, but then opened up with a management statement. After Novy had commented, "That's putting it very mildly," Shafer came in with this remark: "I am interested in Mr. Novy's statement. You say, 'That is putting it very mildly.' " Now here was the crucial issue of negotiations. Management was opening up with strong pressure on this issue. It must have taken self-control for the union not to rush in with a counterattack at the first opening. Yet here was Shafer sitting back and simply asking management to talk more fully and freely on the subject. The result was that the management people did go on at length to lay out their position. They got the satisfaction of a full hearing. Only when they had had their say did the union open up with its arguments. At that time Love talked at length, and management gave him a full hearing.

This brings us up against the most puzzling problem of these negotiations. Somehow during the course of negotiations John Gossett decided he could trust Jake Shafer. When did it happen? We don't know. Probably it was no sudden decision but rather a slowly growing conviction. Why did it happen? No one point will give us the answer, but this point seems to be of considerable importance.

Gossett decided that Shafer had a sincere interest in management's problems. What did Shafer say to get that point across? Was it enough simply to say that he was interested in costs and productivity? Hardly. If union men could win the confidence of management men simply by saying, "I am interested in your problems," the situation (for the union) would be far simpler than what we actually find.

That is what we see in research. If I am discussing my problems with you, I am not satisfied with a statement of your interest. It does not matter whether the statement is a short sentence or a long and eloquent speech. I will only feel that you are interested *if you act interested.* And you can act interested only by encouraging me to explain my problems to you. I will only feel that you understand me and my problems if you help me to explain them fully to you *as I see them.*

I am suggesting that, in negotiations, listening is just as important as talking. In part, Shafer won the confidence of Gossett through listening to him, through giving him a full and sympathetic hearing.

Disagreeing with Respect

Listening is not enough. After you have heard the other man out, if you still disagree, you must have a way of stating that disagreement. Here again there are two contrasting ways of doing it:

1. You can say, in effect, "I think you are wrong. You are wrong for the following reasons:" —and so on with

a systematic "proof" of the other fellow's stupidity.

2. You can say, in effect, "Well, I see why you feel the way you do. In terms of the experience you have had, that is a reasonable point of view. But on the other hand, our experience has been different, and we have different problems." You can then go on to describe your experience and problems in order to show why the proposal is unacceptable.

The first approach leads to people trying to outsmart each other. The "winner" of such an argument simply humiliates his opponent in such a way as to make agreement impossible.

The second approach moves the argument into a field where agreement becomes possible. Relating sentiments to experience is sound science as well as sound strategy. We know that people at different positions and with different functions in an organization have different experiences which naturally build different sentiments. We cannot expect the executive and the union leader to have the same body of experience. But they can ask each other how their experience can be reorganized so that a given proposal will be acceptable to both parties.

In effect, this was the pattern followed on the critical issues in these negotiations. The steps went something like this:

1. An expression of respect for the other fellow's position.

2. A discussion of the body of experience that makes it impossible to accept his proposal.

3. A *joint* exploration of ways in which the proposal

can be changed and/or of the ways in which the experience of the two parties can be changed so as to make such a proposal acceptable.

When negotiations are conducted in this way, mutual respect grows, and the parties actually come to grips with the economic and human relations problems of the plant. They do not get lost in abstract arguments over principles.

• 45 •

Ten Simple Rules[1]

HOWARD WHITMAN

For three years, Professor Wallace Brett Donham of Harvard and associates from other universities did research for their pioneer course in Human Relations—the art of getting along with people.

Here are ten simple rules for keeping out, or getting out, of trouble, distilled for all of us mortals from the rich mash of the professors' collective experiences:

1. Learn all about a problem before trying to solve it. Listen a lot. Talk a little.

2. See the *total situation.* Don't act on just a part of it.

3. Don't be deceived by *logic.* Most problems are full of emotion. Emotions aren't "logical."

4. Watch the meaning of words. Look behind words to get their full impact.

[1] From the article, "How to Keep Out of Trouble," by Howard Whitman in *Collier's*, Sept. 25, 1948, p. 28. Reprinted by permission.

5. No moral judgments, please. Until you have diagnosed a problem don't leap to conclusions about what's *right* and what's *wrong*.

6. Imagine yourself in the other fellow's shoes. See how the problem looks from where he sits.

7. When a problem gets you down, get away from it. Put it in the back of your mind for a week. When you approach it again the solution may be obvious.

8. Ask yourself, "What are the forces acting upon the other fellow? Why does he behave as he does?"

9. *Diagnosis* must come before *action*. Use the doctor's approach. Don't prescribe until you're sure what is wrong.

10. Easy does it. Quick solutions are often the quick route to trouble. Take your time.

• 46 •

In the Laboratory with Agassiz[1]

SAMUEL H. SCUDDER

It was more than fifteen years ago [from 1874] that I entered the laboratory of Professor Agassiz, and told him I had enrolled my name in the Scientific School as a student of natural history. He asked me a few questions about my object in coming, my antecedents generally, the mode in which I afterwards proposed to use the knowledge I might acquire, and, finally, whether I wished to study any special branch. To the latter I replied that, while I wished to be well grounded in all departments of zoology, I purposed to devote myself specially to insects.

"When do you wish to begin?" he asked.

"Now," I replied.

This seemed to please him, and with an energetic "Very well!" he reached from a shelf a huge jar of specimens in yellow alcohol.

[1] *Every Saturday*, April 4, 1874, pp. 369–370.

"Take this fish," said he, "and look at it; we call it a haemulon; by and by I will ask what you have seen."

With that he left me, but in a moment returned with explicit instructions as to the care of the object entrusted to me.

"No man is fit to be a naturalist," said he, "who does not know how to take care of specimens."

I was to keep the fish before me in a tin tray, and occasionally moisten the surface with alcohol from the jar, always taking care to replace the stopper tightly. Those were not the days of ground-glass stoppers and elegantly shaped exhibition jars; all the old students will recall the huge neckless glass bottles with their leaky, wax-besmeared corks, half eaten by insects, and begrimed with cellar dust. Entomology was a cleaner science than ichthyology, but the example of the Professor, who had unhesitatingly plunged to the bottom of the jar to produce the fish, was infectious; and though this alcohol had "a very ancient and fishlike smell," I really dared not show any aversion within these sacred precincts, and treated the alcohol as though it were pure water. Still I was conscious of a passing feeling of disappointment, for gazing at a fish did not commend itself to an ardent entomologist. My friends at home, too, were annoyed, when they discovered that no amount of eau-de-Cologne would drown the perfume which haunted me like a shadow.

In ten minutes I had seen all that could be seen in that fish, and started in search of the Professor—who had, however, left the Museum; and when I returned, after lingering over some of the odd animals stored in the upper apartment, my specimen was dry all over. I dashed the fluid over the fish as if to resuscitate the beast from a fainting-fit, and looked with anxiety for a return of the normal sloppy appearance. This little excitement over, nothing was to be done but to return to a steadfast gaze at my mute companion. Half an hour passed—an hour—another hour; the fish began to look loathsome. I turned it over and around; looked it in the face—ghastly; from behind, beneath, above, sideways, at a three-quarters' view—just as ghastly. I was in despair; at an early hour I concluded that lunch was necessary; so, with infinite relief, the fish was carefully replaced in the jar, and for an hour I was free.

On my return, I learned that Professor Agassiz had been at the Museum, but had gone, and would not return for several hours. My fellow-students were too busy to be disturbed by continued conversation. Slowly I drew forth that hideous fish, and with a feeling of desperation again looked at it. I might not use a magnifying-glass; instruments of all kinds were interdicted. My two hands, my two eyes, and the fish: it seemed a most limited field. I pushed my finger down its throat to feel how sharp the teeth were. I began to count the scales in the different rows, until I was convinced that that was nonsense. At last a happy thought struck me—I would draw the fish; and now with surprise I began to discover new features in the creature. Just then the Professor returned.

"That is right," said he; "a pencil is one of the best of eyes. I am glad to notice, too, that you keep your specimen wet, and your bottle corked."

With these encouraging words, he added:

"Well, what is it like?"

He listened attentively to my brief rehearsal of the structure of parts whose names were still unknown to me: the fringed gill-arches and movable operculum; the pores of the head, fleshy lips and lidless eyes; the lateral line, the spinous fins and forked tail; the compressed and arched body. When I had finished, he waited as if expecting more, and then, with an air of disappointment:

"You have not looked very carefully; why," he continued more earnestly, "you haven't even seen one of the most conspicuous features of the animal, which is as plainly before your eyes as the fish itself; look again, look again!" and he left me to my misery.

I was piqued; I was mortified. Still more of that wretched fish! But now I set myself to my task with a will, and discovered one new thing after another, until I saw how just the Professor's criticism had been. The afternoon passed quickly; and when, toward its close, the Professor inquired:

"Do you see it yet?"

"No," I replied, "I am certain I do not, but I see how little I saw before."

"That is next best," said he, earnestly, "but I won't hear you now; put away your fish and go home; perhaps you will be ready with a better answer in the morning. I will examine you before you look at the fish."

This was disconcerting. Not only must I think of my fish all night, studying, without the object before me, what this unknown but most visible feature might be; but also, without reviewing my new discoveries, I must give an exact account of them the next day. I had a bad memory; so I walked home by Charles River in a distracted state, with my two perplexities.

The cordial greeting from the Professor the next morning was reassuring; here was a man who seemed to be quite as anxious as I that I should see for myself what he saw.

"Do you perhaps mean," I asked, "that the fish has symmetrical sides with paired organs?"

His thoroughly pleased "Of course! of course!" repaid the wakeful hours of the previous night. After he had discoursed most happily and enthusiastically—as he always did—upon the importance of this point, I ventured to ask what I should do next.

"Oh, look at your fish!" he said, and left me again to my own devices. In a little more than an hour he returned, and heard my new catalogue.

"That is good, that is good!" he repeated; "but that is not all; go on"; and so for three long days he placed that fish before my eyes, forbidding me to look at anything else, or to use any artificial aid. "Look, look, look," was his repeated injunction.

This was the best entomological lesson I ever had—a lesson whose influence has extended to the details of every subsequent study; a legacy the Professor has left to me, as he has left it to many others, of inestimable value, which we could not buy, with which we cannot part.

A year afterward, some of us were amusing ourselves with chalking outlandish beasts on the Museum blackboard. We drew prancing starfishes; frogs in mortal combat; hydraheaded worms; stately crawfishes, standing on their tails, bearing aloft umbrellas; and grotesque fishes with gaping mouths and staring eyes. The Professor came in shortly after, and was as amused as any at our experiments. He looked at the fishes.

"Haemulons, every one of them," he said; "Mr. ——— drew them."

True; and to this day, if I attempt a fish, I can draw nothing but haemulons.

The fourth day, a second fish of the same group was placed beside the first, and I was bidden to point out the resemblances and differences between the two; another and another followed, until the entire family lay before me, and a whole legion of jars covered the table and surrounding shelves; the odor had become a pleasant perfume; and even now, the sight of an old, six-inch, worm-eaten cork brings fragrant memories.

The whole group of haemulons was thus brought in review; and, whether engaged upon the dissection of the internal organs, the preparation and examination of the bony framework, or the description of the various parts, Agassiz's training in the method of observing facts and their orderly arrangement was ever accompanied by the urgent exhortation not to be content with them.

"Facts are stupid things," he would say, "until brought into connection with some general law."

At the end of eight months, it was almost with reluctance that I left these friends and turned to insects; but what I had gained by this outside experience has been of greater value than years of later investigation in my favorite groups.

• 47 •

Hypotheses[1]

THOMAS HENRY HUXLEY

WHEN our means of observation of any natural fact fail to carry us beyond a certain point, it is perfectly legitimate, and often extremely useful, to make a supposition as to what we should see, if we could carry direct observation a step further. A supposition of this kind is what is called a *hypothesis*, and the value of any hypothesis depends upon the extent to which reasoning upon the assumption that it is true enables us to explain or account for the phenomena with which it is concerned.

Thus, if a person is standing close behind you, and you suddenly feel a blow on your back, you have no direct evidence of the cause of the blow; and if you two were alone, you could not possibly obtain any; but you immediately suppose that this person has struck you. Now that is a hypothesis, and it is a legitimate hypothesis, first, because it explains the fact; and secondly, be-

[1] From *Introductory to Science Primers,* 1884.

cause no other explanation is probable; probable meaning in accordance with the ordinary course of nature. If your companion declared that you fancied you felt a blow, or that some invisible spirit struck you, you would probably decline to accept his explanation of the fact. You would say that both the hypotheses by which he professed to explain the phenomenon were extremely improbable; or in other words, that in the ordinary course of nature fancies of this kind do not occur, nor spirits strike blows. In fact, his hypotheses would be illegitimate, and yours would be legitimate; and, in all probability, you would act upon your own. In daily life, nine-tenths of our actions are based upon suppositions or hypotheses, and our success or failure in practical affairs depends upon the legitimacy of these hypotheses. You believe a man on the hypothesis that he is always truthful; you give him pecuniary credit on the hypothesis that he is solvent.

Thus, everybody invents, and, indeed, is compelled to invent, hypotheses in order to account for phenomena of the cause of which he was no direct evidence; and they are just as legitimate and necessary in science as in common life. Only the scientific reasoner must be careful to remember that which is sometimes forgotten in daily life, that a hypothesis must be regarded as a means and not as an end; that we may cherish it so long as it helps us to explain the order of nature; but that we are bound to throw it away without hesitation as soon as it is shown to be inconsistent with any part of that order.

• 48 •

Agreement and Disagreement[1]

ALFRED KORZYBSKI

AN IMPORTANT aspect of the problem of existence can be made clear by some examples. Let us recall that a noise or written sign, to become a symbol, must stand for *something*. Let us imagine that you, my reader, and myself are engaged in an argument. Before us, on the table, lies something which we usually call a box of matches: you argue that there are matches in this box; I say that there are no matches in it. Our argument can be settled. We open the box and look, and both become convinced. It must be noticed that in our argument we used *words*, because they stood for something; so when we began to argue, the argument could be solved to our mutual satisfaction, since there was a *third* factor, the object, which corresponded to the symbol used, and this settled the dispute. A third factor was present, and agreement became possible. Let us

[1] From *Science and Sanity: An Introduction to Non-Aristotelian Systems and General Semantics*, Lakeville, Connecticut, The International Non-Aristotelian Library Publishing Co., 1933, pp. 81–82, 418–420 (3d ed., 1948). Reprinted by permission.

take another example. Let us try to settle the problem: "Is blah-blah a case of tra-tra?" Let us assume that you say "yes," and that I say "no." Can we reach any agreement? It is a real tragedy, of which life is full, that such an argument cannot be solved at all. We used noises, not words. There was *no third* factor for which these noises stood as symbols, and so we could argue endlessly without any possibility of agreement. That the noises may have stood for some *semantic* disturbance is quite a different problem, and in such a case a psychopathologist should be consulted, but arguments should stop. The reader will have no difficulty in gathering from daily life other examples, many of them of highly tragic character. . . .

Let us begin with a Smith who knows nothing of what has been said here, and who is *not* conscious of abstracting. For him, as well as for Fido, there is, in principle, no realization of the "Characteristics left out." He is "emotionally" convinced that his words entirely cover the "object" which "*is* so and so." He identifies his lower abstractions with characteristics left out, with higher abstractions which have all characteristics included. He ascribes to words an entirely false value and certitude which they cannot have. He does not realize that his words may have different meanings for the other fellow. He ascribes to words "emotional" *objectivity* and value, and the verbal, aristotelian "permanence," "definiteness," "one-value," to objects. When he hears something that he does not like, he does not ask "what do you mean?" but, under the semantic pressure of identification, he ascribes his own meanings to the other fellow's words. For him, words "*are*" "emotionally" overloaded, objectified semantic fetishes, even as to the primitive man who believed in the "magic of words." Upon hearing anything strange, his *semantic reaction* is undelayed and may appear as, "I disagree with you," or "I don't believe you." There is no reason to be dramatic about any unwelcome statement. One needs definitions and interpretations of such statements, which probably are correct from the speaker's point of view, if we grant him his informations, *his undefined terms,* the structure of his language and premises which build up his *semantic reactions.* But our Smith, innocent of the "structure of human knowledge," has mostly a semantic belief in the one-value, absoluteness, of things, and thinghood of words, and does not know, or does not *remember,* that words *are not* the events themselves. Words represent higher order abstractions manufactured by higher nerve centres, and objects represent lower order abstractions manufactured by lower nerve centres. Under such *identity-delusions,* he becomes an absolutist, a dogmatist, a finalist. He seeks to establish "ultimate truths," "eternal verities," and is willing to fight for them, never knowing or remembering, otherwise forgetting, the "characteristics left out"; never recognizing that the noises he makes *are not* the objective actualities we deal with. If somebody contradicts him, he is much disturbed. Forgetting characteristics left out, he is always "right." For him his statement is not only *the* only statement possible, but he actually attributes some cosmic objective evaluation to it.

The above *description* is unsatisfactory, but cannot be much improved upon, since the situation involves *unspeakable* affective components which *are not* words. We must simply try to put ourselves in his place, and to live through his experiences when he identifies and believes without question that his words "*are*" the things they only stand for. To give the full consequences of such identification resulting in wrong evaluation, I might add most tedious *descriptions* of the interplay of situations, evaluations, in quarrels, unhappinesses, disagreements, leading to dramas and tragedies, as well as to many forms of "mental" illness effectively described only in the *belles-lettres*. Thus, $Smith_1$, who is *not* conscious of abstracting, makes the statement, "A circle is not square." Let us suppose that $Brown_1$ contradicts him. $Smith_1$ is angered; for his *semantic reactions*, his statement "is" the "plain truth," and $Brown_1$ must be a fool. He objectifies it, ascribes to it undue value. For him, it "is" "experience," a "fact," and he bursts into speech, denouncing $Brown_1$ and showing how wrong he "is." From this semantic attitude, many difficulties and tragedies arise.

But if $Smith_2$ (conscious of abstracting) makes the statement, "A circle is not square," and $Brown_2$ contradicts him, what would $Smith_2$ do? He would smile, would not burst into speech to defend *his* statement, but would ask $Brown_2$, "What do you mean? I do not quite understand you." After receiving some answer, $Smith_2$ would explain to $Brown_2$ that his statement is not anything to quarrel about, as it is verbal and is true only by *definition*. He would also grant the right of

$Brown_2$ *not* to accept his *definition*, but to use another one to satisfy himself. The problem would then, naturally, arise as to what definition both could accept, or which would be generally acceptable. And the problem would then be solved by purely pragmatic considerations. Words appear as creatures of definitions, and optional; but this attitude involves important and new *semantic reactions*.

This fact seems of tremendous semantic importance, as it provides the working foundation for a theory of "universal agreement." In the first part of the above example, $Smith_1$, according to the accepted standards, was "right" ("a circle is not square"). Is he "more right" than $Brown_1$, for whom the "circle is square?" Not at all. Both statements belong to the verbal level, and represent only forms of representation for *semantic reactions inside their skin*. Either may be "right" by some explicit or implicit "definitions." Are the two statements equally valid? This *we do not know a priori*; we must investigate to find out if the noises uttered have meanings outside of pathology, or which statement structurally covers the situation better, carries us structurally further in describing and analysing this world. Only scientific structural analysis can give the preference to one form over another. Smith and Brown can only produce their "definitions" according to their *semantic reactions*, but they are *not* judges as to which "definitions" will *ultimately* stand the test of structure.

• 49 •

Definition of a Gentleman[1]

JOHN HENRY NEWMAN

IT IS almost a definition of a gentleman to say he is one who never inflicts pain. This description is both refined and, as far as it goes, accurate. He is mainly occupied in merely removing the obstacles which hinder the free and unembarrassed action of those about him, and he concurs with their movements rather than takes the initiative himself. His benefits may be considered as parallel to what are called comforts or conveniences in arrangements of a personal nature; like an easy chair or a good fire, which do their part in dispelling cold and fatigue, though nature provides both means of rest and animal heat without them.

The true gentleman in like manner carefully avoids whatever may cause a jar or a jolt in the minds of those with whom he is cast—all clashing of opinion, or collision of feeling, all restraint or suspicion or gloom or resentment; his great concern being to make everyone at ease and at home. He has his eyes on all his company;

[1] From *The Idea of a University*, 1852.

he is tender towards the bashful, gentle towards the distant, and merciful towards the absurd. He can recollect to whom he is speaking; he guards against unreasonable allusions or topics which may irritate. He is seldom prominent in conversation and never wearisome. He makes light of favors while he does them, and seems to be receiving when he is conferring. He never speaks of himself except when compelled, never defends himself by a mere retort. He has no ears for slander or gossip, is scrupulous in imputing motives to those who interfere with him, and interprets everything for the best. He is never mean or little in his disputes, never takes unfair advantage, never mistakes personalities or sharp sayings for arguments, or insinuates evil which he dare not say out. From a long-sighted prudence, he observes the maxim of the ancient sage, that we should ever conduct ourselves toward our enemy as if he were one day to be our friend.

He has too much good sense to be affronted at insults, he is too well employed to remember injuries, and too indolent to bear malice. He is patient, forbearing, and resigned on philosophical principles: he submits to pain because it is inevitable, to bereavement because it is irreparable, and to death because it is his destiny. If he engages in controversy of any kind, his disciplined intellect preserves him from the blundering discourtesy of better, perhaps, but less educated minds who, like blunt weapons, tear and hack instead of cutting clean, who mistake the point in argument, waste their strength on trifles, misconceive their adversary, and leave the question more involved than they find it.

He may be right or wrong in his opinion but he is too clear headed to be unjust. He is simple as he is forcible, and as brief as he is decisive. Nowhere shall we find greater candor, consideration, indulgence; he throws himself into the minds of his opponents, he accounts for their mistakes. He knows the weakness of human reason as well as its strength, its province and its limits.

If he be an unbeliever, he will be too profound and large-minded to ridicule religion or to act against it; he is too wise to be a dogmatist or fanatic in his infidelity. He respects piety and devotion; he even supports institutions as venerable, beautiful, or useful, to which he does not assent; he honors the ministers of religion, and it contents him to decline its mysteries without assailing or denouncing them. He is a friend of religious toleration, and that, not only because his philosophy has taught him to look on all forms of faith with an impartial eye, but also from the gentleness and effeminacy of feeling which is the attendant on civilization.